AMERICA'S ALL-TIME FAVORITE SONGS

FOR GOD AND COUNTRY

178 BEST-LOVED SONGS
FULL PIANO ARRANGEMENTS WITH CHORDS AND LYRICS
COMPILED AND EDITED BY AMY APPLEBY

EXCLUSIVELY DISTRIBUTED BY

HAL•LEONARD®

This book is dedicated to all who serve in the United States Armed Forces

Cover photograph: Comstock Images
Project editor: Felipe Orozco

This book Copyright © 2006, 2008 by Amsco Publications,

Order No. AM 994950
International Standard Book Number: 978-0-8256-3667-7

PREFACE

Americans are a decidedly musical people who take pride in traditional values and cultural diversity. For this reason, we are many times blessed with a rich song heritage. Our national songbag is positively brimming with music that expresses every aspect of daily life—in peacetime and at war. In fact, it has been said that the whole tumultuous and glorious history of the United States may best be learned from her songbooks.

Like today's digital music generation, Americans of yesteryear had a true passion for music. Writing, singing, and listening to songs were popular national pastimes—and trading songs with family and friends was a central part of home and village life.

Songs have been a chief national product of our country since the first printing presses were set up in colonial America. During the first year of the Civil War alone, over two thousand songs were published in the United States. These heartfelt anthems, rousing marches, and beautiful hymns inspired courage and strength in the armies of both North and South. Music was so instrumental to the war effort that General Robert E. Lee once said: "Without music, there would have been no army." During Reconstruction, this music served to heal the wounds of war, and reunify the battle-scarred nation. So powerful was their effect on the hearts of the people, that these songs are still as vibrant today as they were on the battlefield so many years ago.

This comprehensive collection tells the story of America's enduring faith in God and love of country, now spanning four centuries. Here you will find the most treasured patriotic anthems, devotional hymns, heart songs, gospel music, and spirituals of our nation. Also included are official songs of the United States, as well as songs of special importance to the men and women in the military (to whom this book is respectfully dedicated).

Whenever you play or sing the great songs in this volume, you celebrate a truly great American tradition. Share these wonderful songs with others and you keep the tradition alive.

CONTENTS

CELEBRATE AMERICA

FROM SEA TO SHINING SEA

FOR OUR SOLDIERS

FOR OUR SAILORS AND FLYERS

ON THE HOMEFRONT

FOR THE FALLEN

HYMNS AND PRAYERS

BELOVED SPIRITUALS

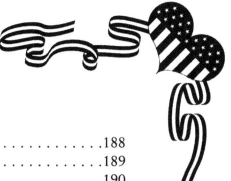

GOSPEL PRAISE

SACRED CLASSICS

HOME FOR THE HOLIDAYS

CELEBRATE AMERICA

10

America
(My Country 'Tis of Thee)

Words by Samuel Francis Smith
English anthem "God Save the King"

Moderately slow

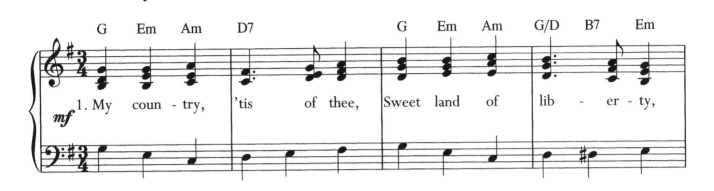

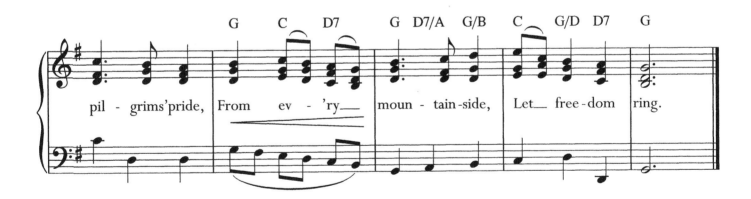

2. My native country, thee,
Land of the noble free,
Thy name I love.
I love thy rocks and rills,
Thy woods and templed hills;
My heart with rapture thrills
Like that above.

3. Let music swell the breeze,
And ring from all the trees,
Sweet freedom's song.
Let mortal tongues awake,
Let all that breathe partake,
Let rocks their silence break,
The sound prolong.

4. Our fathers' God, to Thee,
Author of liberty,
To Thee we sing.
Long may our land be bright
With freedom's holy light,
Protect us by Thy might,
Great God, our King.

★★★★★★★★★★★★★★★★★★★★★★★★★★★★★★★★★★★

The American Flag

Words by Joseph Rodman Drake
Music by John W. Tufts

With spirit

2. Flag of the free heart's hope and home,
   By angel hands to valor giv'n,
   Thy stars have lit the welkin dome,
   And all thy hues were born in heav'n
   And all thy hues were born in heaven.

3. Forever float that standard sheet,
   Where breathes the foe but falls before us,
   With Freedom's soil beneath our feet,
   And freedom's banner streaming o'er us,
   And freedom's banner streaming o'er us.

☆☆☆☆☆☆☆☆☆☆☆☆ ☆ The American Flag ☆☆☆☆☆☆☆☆☆☆☆☆

America, the Beautiful

Words by Katherine Lee Bates
Music by Samuel A. Ward

Moderately

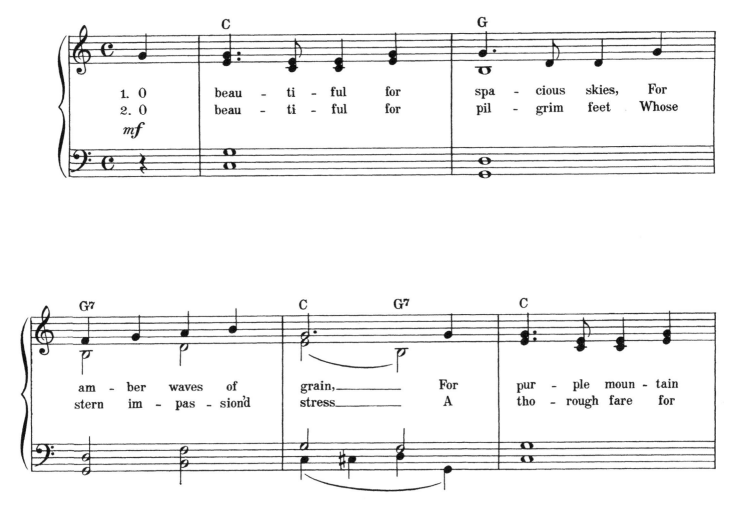

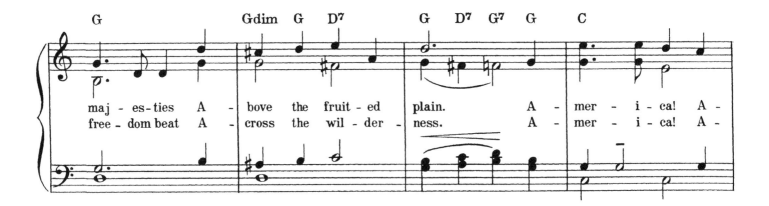

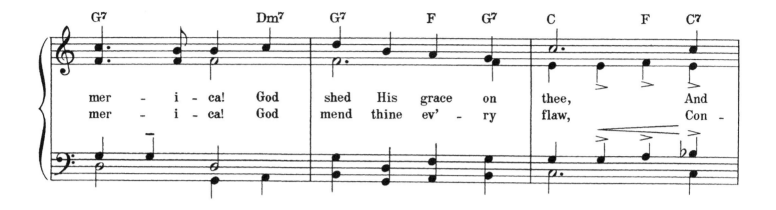

mer - i - ca! God shed His grace on thee, And
mer - i - ca! God mend thine ev' - ry flaw, Con -

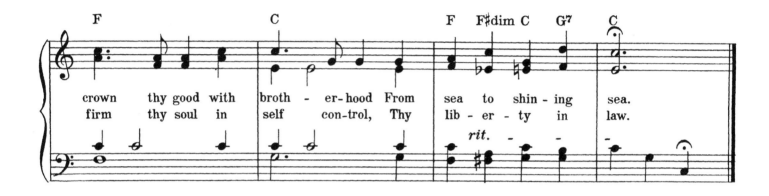

crown thy good with broth - er-hood From sea to shin - ing sea.
firm thy soul in self con-trol, Thy lib - er - ty in law.

3. O beautiful for heros prov'd
In liberating strife,
Who more than self their country loved,
And mercy more than life.
America! America!
May God thy gold refine
Till all success be nobleness,
And ev'ry gain divine.

4. O beautiful for patriot dream,
That sees beyond the years,
Thine alabaster cities gleam
Undimmed by human tears.
America! America!
God shed His grace on thee,
And crown thy good with brotherhood,
From sea to shining sea.

Battle Hymn of the Republic
(Glory Hallelujah)

Words by Julia Ward Howe
American folk song "John Brown's Body"

With spirit

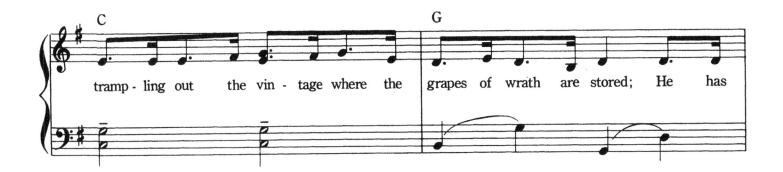

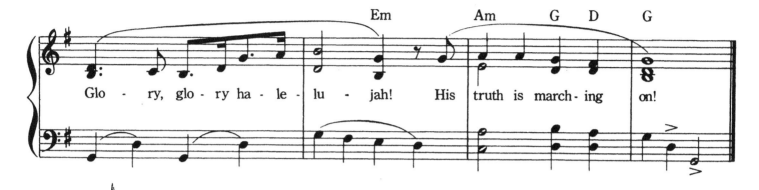

Glo - ry, glo - ry ha - le - lu - jah! His truth is march - ing on!

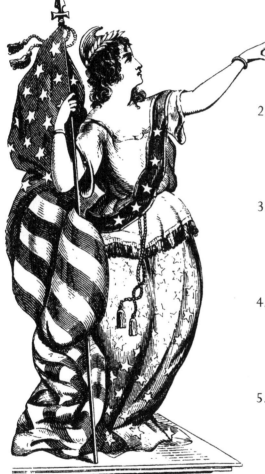

2. I have seen Him in the watchfires of a hundred circling camps,
They have builded Him an altar in the evening dews and damps,
I can read His righteous sentence by the dim and flaring lamps,
His day is marching on.
Refrain

3. I have read a fiery gospel writ in burnished rows of steel:
"As ye deal with My contemners, so with you My grace shall deal."
Let the Hero, born of woman, crush the serpent with His heel,
Since God is marching on.
Refrain

4. He has sounded forth the trumpet that shall never call retreat,
He is sifting out the hearts of men before His judgment seat.
Oh, be swift, my soul, to answer Him, be jubilant, my feet!
Our God is marching on.
Refrain

5. In the beauty of the lilies, Christ was born across the sea,
With a glory in his bosom that transfigures you and me.
As He died to make men holy, let us die to make men free,
While God is marching on.
Refrain

Flag of the Free

Words by J.P. McCaskey
Music by Richard Wagner
"Bridal Chorus" from *Lohengrin*

Moderately slow

1. Flag of the free! fair - est to see!

Borne through the strife and the thun - der of war, Ban - ner so

bright with star - ry light, Float ev - er

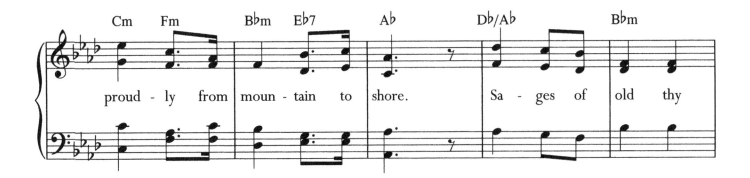

proud - ly from moun - tain to shore. Sa - ges of old thy

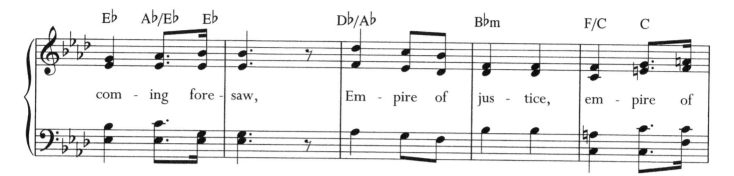

coming fore- saw, Em - pire of jus - tice, em - pire of

law; Flag of our fa - thers! round_ all the world,__

Blest of the mil - lions wher - ev - er un - furled;__ Ter - ror to

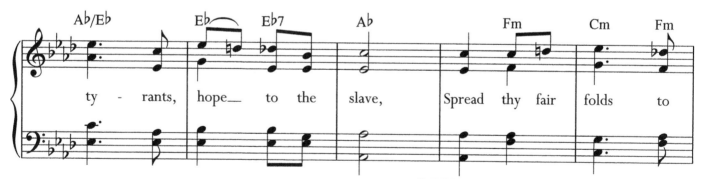

ty - rants, hope_ to the slave, Spread thy fair folds to

REFRAIN

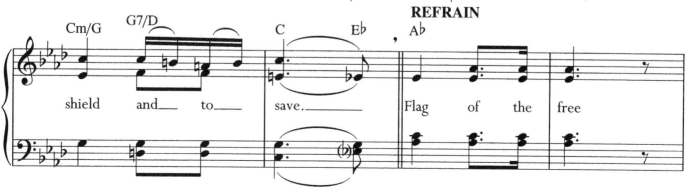

shield and_ to_ save.__ Flag of the free

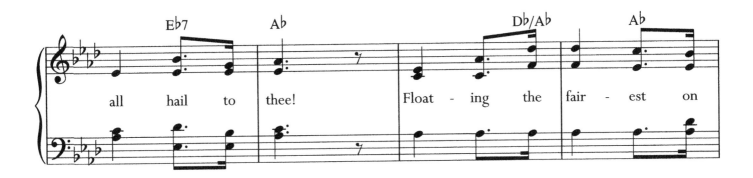

all hail to thee! Float - ing the fair - est on

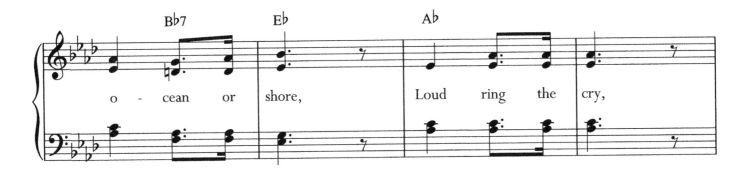

o - cean or shore, Loud ring the cry,

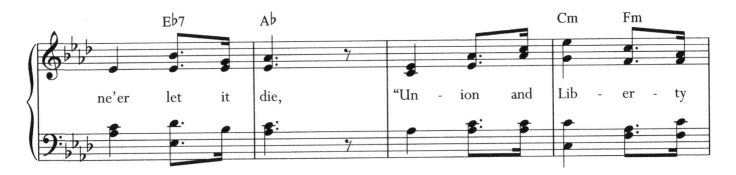

ne'er let it die, "Un - ion and Lib - er - ty

1., 2. now, ev - er-more!" **3.** now, ev - er- more!"

2. Flag of the free! all turn to thee,
   Golden thy stars in the blue of their sky!
   Flag of the brave! onward to save,
   Crimson thy bars floating gaily on high!
   Splendid thy story, mighty to save,
   Matchless thy beauty on land or wave,
   Heroes have borne thee aloft in the fray,
   Foemen who scorn'd thee have all pass'd away;
   Pride of our country, hail'd from afar,
   Banner of Promise, lose not a star.
   Refrain

3. Flag of the brave, long may it wave!
   Chosen of God while His might we adore,
   High in the van, for manhood of man,
   Symbol of right through the years passing o'er;
   Flow'r of the ages, promised of yore,
   Flow'r of the ages, fade nevermore!
   Emblem of freedom, "Many in One,"
   O'er thee thine eagle, bird of the sun;
   All hail, "Old Glory!" hearts leap to see
   How from the nations the world looks to thee.
   Refrain

God Save America

Words by William G. Ballantine
Music by Alexis F. Lvov

2. God save America! Here may all races
   Mingle together as children of God,
   Founding an empire on brotherly kindness,
   Equal in liberty, made of one blood!

3. God save America! Brotherhood banish
   Wail of the worker and curse of the crushed;
   Joy break in songs from her jubilant millions,
   Hailing the day when all discords are hushed!

4. God save America! Bearing the olive,
   Hers be the blessing the peacemakers prove,
   Calling the nations to glad federation,
   Leading the world in the triumph of love!

5. God save America! 'Mid all her splendors,
   Save her from pride and from luxury;
   Throne in her heart the unseen and eternal;
   Right be her might and the truth make her free!

Hail, Columbia

Words by Joseph Hopkinson
Music by Philip Phile

Majestically

1. Hail, Co-lum-bia, hap-py land, ___ Hail ye he-roes, Heav'n born band, Who
2. Im-mor-tal pa-triots rise once more, De-fend your rights, de-fend your shores, Let

fought and bled in Free-dom's cause, Who fought and bled in Free-dom's cause, And
no rude foe with im-pi-ous hand, Let no rude foe with im-pi-ous hand, In-

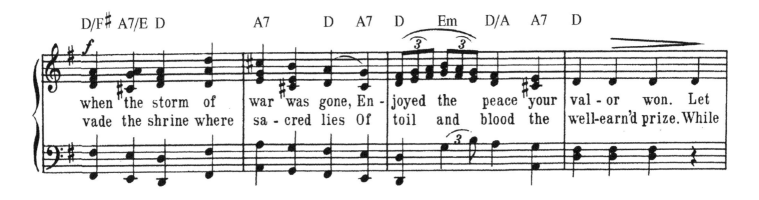

when the storm of war was gone, En-joyed the peace your val-or won. Let
vade the shrine where sa-cred lies Of toil and blood the well-earn'd prize. While

in-de-pend-ence be ___ our boast, ___ Ev-er mind-ful what it cost, ___
off-'ring peace sin-cere and just, In Heav'n we place a man-ly trust, That

Ev - er grate - ful for the prize, — Let its al - tar reach the skies.
truth and jus - tice will pre - vail, And ev -'ry scheme of bond-age fail.

REFRAIN

Firm, u - ni - ted let us be, Rally - ing 'round our lib - er - ty;

As a land of broth - ers joined, Peace and safe - ty we shall find.

3. Sound, sound the trump of fame!
   Let Washington's great name
   Ring through the world with loud applause,
   Ring through the world with loud applause,
   Let every clime to freedom dear
   Listen with a joyful ear.
   With equal skill, with godlike pow'r,
   He governs in the fearful hour
   Of horrid war, or guides with ease
   The happier times of honest peace.
   Refrain

4. Behold, the Chief who now commands,
   Once more to serve his country stands,
   The rock on which the storm will beat;
   The rock on which the storm will beat;
   But armed in virtue, firm and true
   His hopes are fixed on heav'n and you.
   When hope was sinking in dismay,
   When gloom obscured Columbia's day,
   His steady mind, from changes free,
   Resolved on death or liberty.
   Refrain

Hail to the Chief
(The President's March)

Words by Sir Walter Scott
Music by James Sanderson

With spirit

1. Hail to the chief, who in tri - umph ad - van - ces,

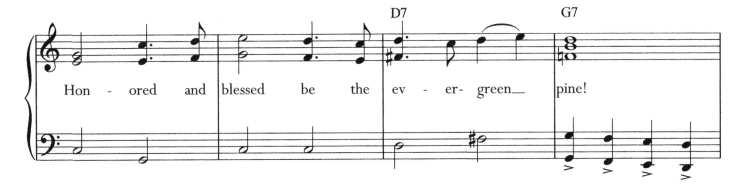

Hon - ored and blessed be the ev - er- green__ pine!

Long may the tree in his ban - ner that glan - ces,

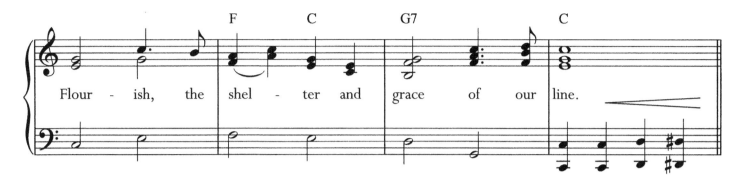

Flour - ish, the shel - ter and grace of our line.

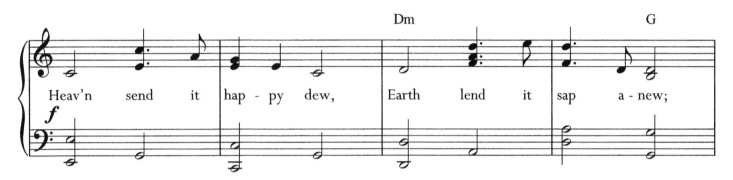

Heav'n send it hap - py dew, Earth lend it sap a - new;

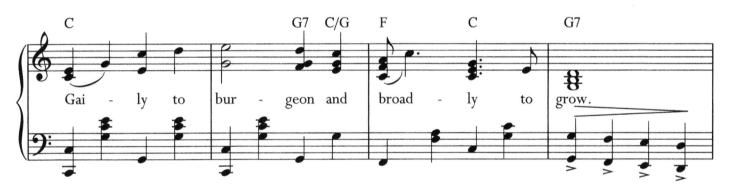

Gai - ly to bur - geon and broad - ly to grow.

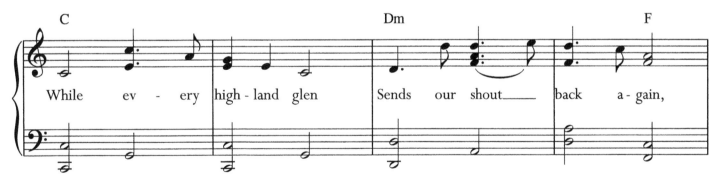

While ev - ery high - land glen Sends our shout_____ back a - gain,

"Rod - er-igh Vich Al - pine dhu ho! i - e - roe!" | roe!"

Rally Round the Flag

Words and music by George F. Root

Energetically

1. Yes, we'll ral - ly round the flag, boys, we'll ral - ly once a - gain,
2. We are spring - ing to the call, Of our broth - ers gone be - fore,

Shout - ing the bat - tle - cry of free - dom, We will ral - ly from the hill - side, we'll
Shout - ing the bat - tle - cry of free - dom, And we'll fill the va - cant ranks With a

REFRAIN

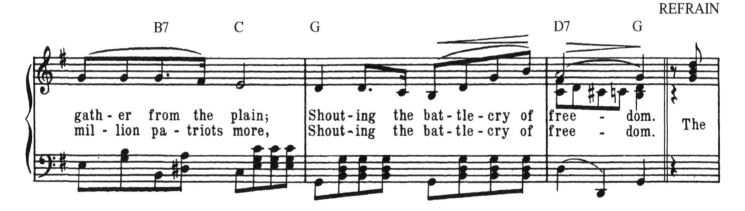

gath - er from the plain; Shout - ing the bat - tle - cry of free - dom.
mil - lion pa - triots more, Shout - ing the bat - tle - cry of free - dom. The

Un - ion for - ev - er, Hur - rah! boys, Hur - rah! Bright in its glo - ry

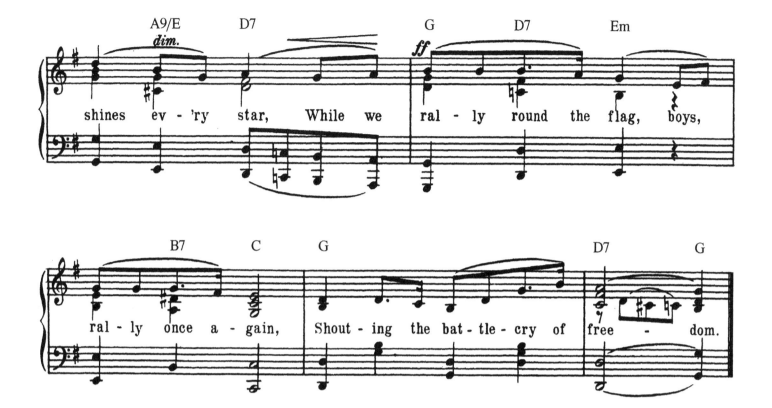

shines ev - 'ry star, While we ral - ly round the flag, boys, ral - ly once a - gain, Shout - ing the bat - tle - cry of free - dom.

3. We will welcome to our numbers
   The loyal, true, and brave,
   Shouting the battle cry of freedom,
   And although they may be poor,
   Not a man shall be a slave,
   Shouting the battle cry of freedom.
   Refrain

Speed Our Republic
(Keller's American Hymn)

Words and music by Matthias Keller

Majestically

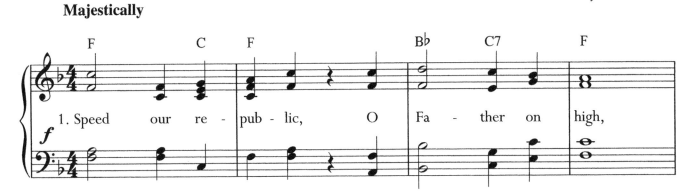

1. Speed our re - pub - lic, O Fa - ther on high,

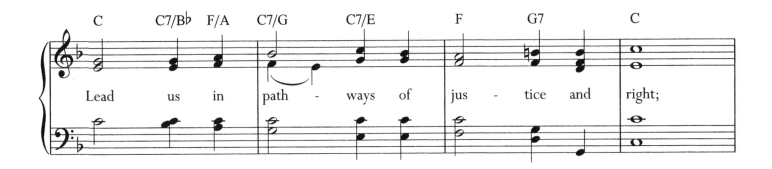

Lead us in path - ways of jus - tice and right;

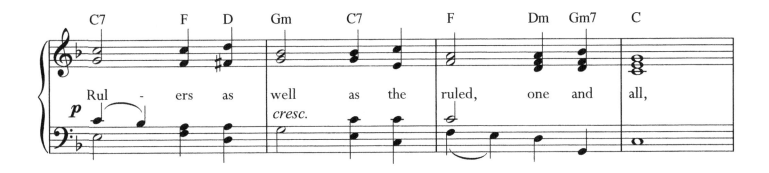

Rul - ers as well as the ruled, one and all,

cresc.

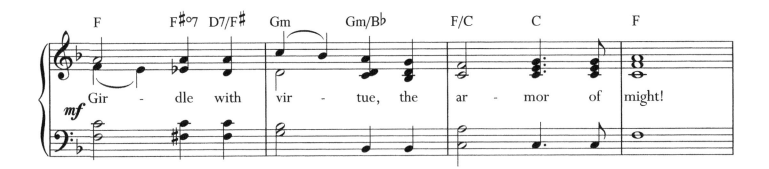

Gir - dle with vir - tue, the ar - mor of might!

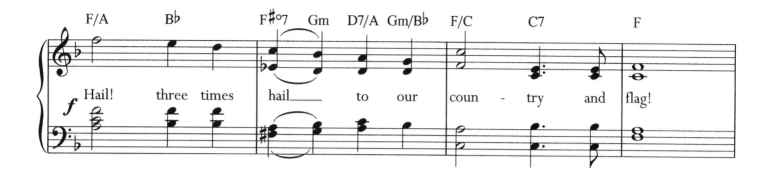

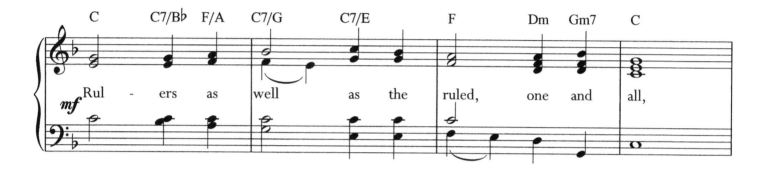

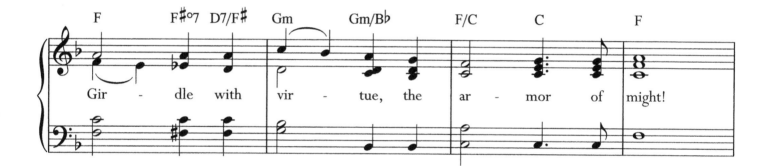

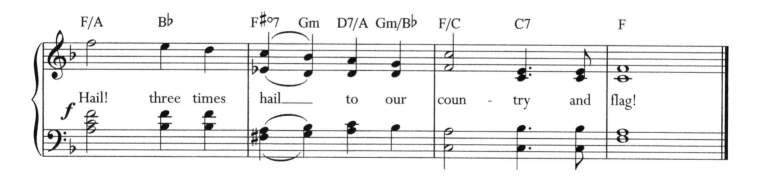

2. Foremost in battle, for freedom to stand,
   We rush to arms when aroused by its call;
   Still as of yore when George Washington led,
   Thunders our war cry, "We conquer or fall!"
   Hail! three times hail to our country and flag!
   Still as of yore when George Washington led,
   Thunders our war cry, "We conquer or fall!"
   Hail! three times hail to our country and flag!

3. Rise up, proud eagle, rise up to the clouds,
   Spread thy broad wing o'er this fair western world!
   Fling from thy beak our dear banner of old!
   Show that it still is for freedom unfurled!
   Hail! three times hail to our country and flag!
   Fling from thy beak our dear banner of old!
   Show that it still is for freedom unfurled!
   Hail! three times hail to our country and flag!

The Stars and Stripes Forever

Words and music by John Philip Sousa

With a steady beat

Hur - rah for the flag of the free!_____ May it

wave as our stan - dard for - ev - er, The

gem of the land and the sea,_____ The_____

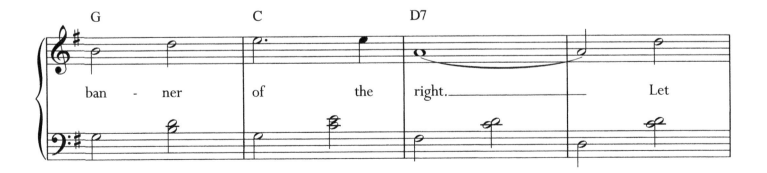

ban - ner of the right._____ Let

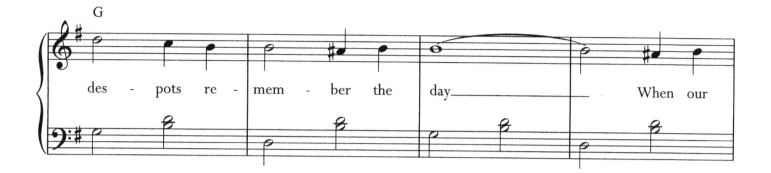

des - pots re - mem - ber the day_____ When our

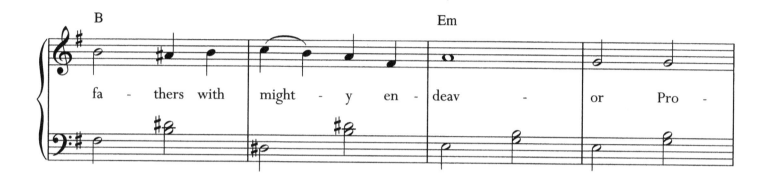

fa - thers with might - y en - deav - or Pro -

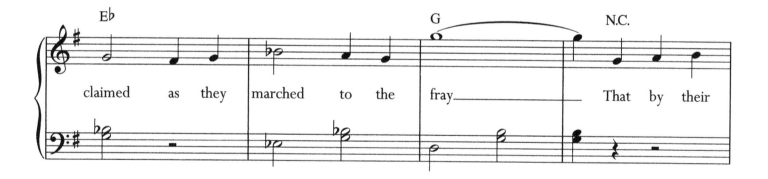

claimed as they marched to the fray_____ That by their

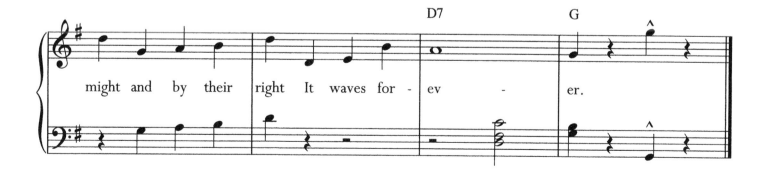

might and by their right It waves for - ev - er.

The Star-Spangled Banner

Words by Francis Scott Key
Music by John Stafford Smith

Energetically

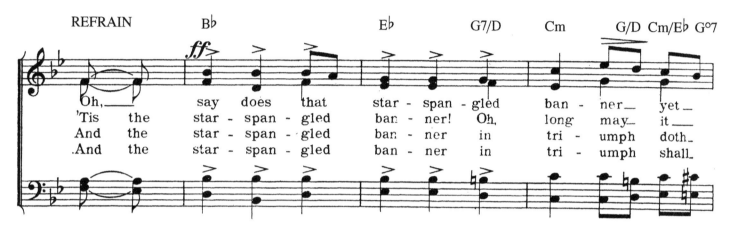

There Are Many Flags in Many Lands

Words and music by Mary H. Howliston

Moderately

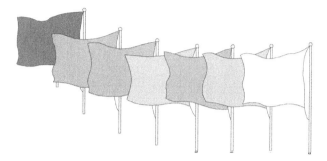 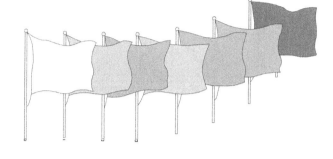

2. I know where the prettiest colors are,
   And I'm sure if I only knew
   How to get them here I'd make a flag
   Of glorious Red, White, and Blue.
   Refrain

3. I would cut a piece from an evening sky,
   Where the stars are shining through,
   And use it, just as it is on high,
   For my stars and field of blue.
   Refrain

4. Then I'd want a piece of a fleecy cloud,
   And some red from a rainbow bright;
   And put them together, side by side,
   For my stripes of red and white.
   Refrain

5. We shall always love the Stars and Stripes,
   And we mean to be ever true
   To this land of ours and the dear old flag,
   The Red, the White, the Blue.
   Refrain

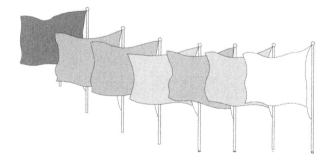 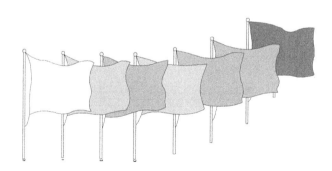

You're a Grand Old Flag

Words and music by George M. Cohan

Moderately fast

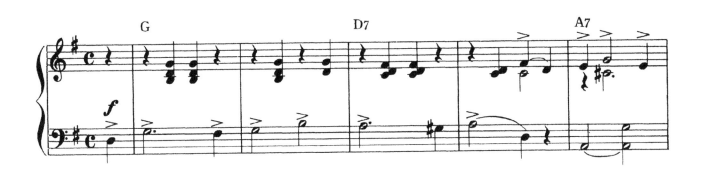

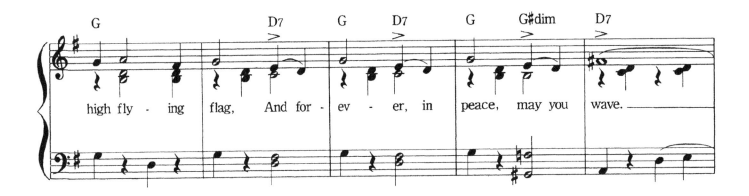

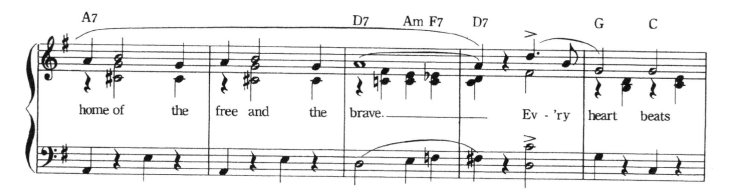

Wave, Wave, Wave

Words and music by John W. Tufts

With a steady beat

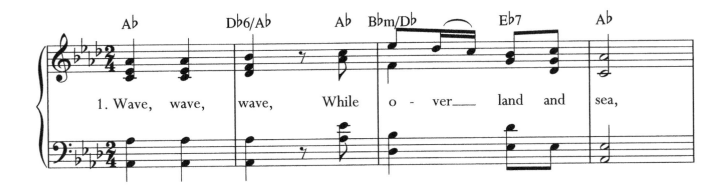

1. Wave, wave, wave, While o - ver___ land and sea,

Waves our glad song to thee, Flag of the no - ble free;

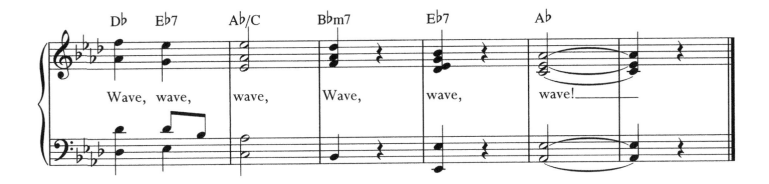

Wave, wave, wave, Wave, wave, wave!___

2. Wave, wave, wave,
   Float high above the trees;
   Fly on the ocean breeze,
   Over the western seas;
   Wave, wave, wave,
   Wave, wave, wave!

3. Wave, wave, wave,
   All thy bright stars in view,
   Stars to the country true,
   Wave in the heavens blue;
   Wave, wave, wave,
   Wave, wave, wave!

FROM SEA TO SHINING SEA

Across the Wide Missouri

(Oh Shenandoah)

American folk song

Freely

Oh Shen-an-doah, I long to hear you, Way hay, you roll-ing

riv - er! Oh, Shen - an - doah, I can't be near you, Way

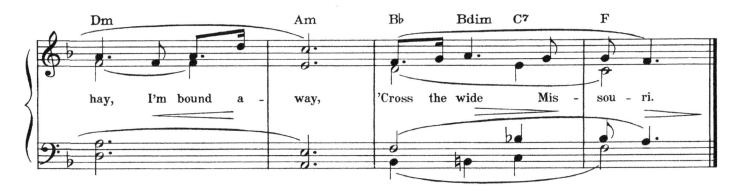

hay, I'm bound a - way, 'Cross the wide Mis - sou - ri.

2. Oh Shenandoah, I love your daughter,
Way hay, you rolling river!
For her I'd cross your roaming water,
Way hay, I'm bound away,
'Cross the wide Missouri.

3. Oh Shenandoah, I'm bound to leave you,
Way hay, you rolling river!
Oh Shenandoah, I'll not deceive you,
Way hay, I'm bound away,
'Cross the wide Missouri.

Alabama
(State Song of Alabama)

Words by Julia Tutwiler
Music by Edna Gockel-Gussen

Moderately

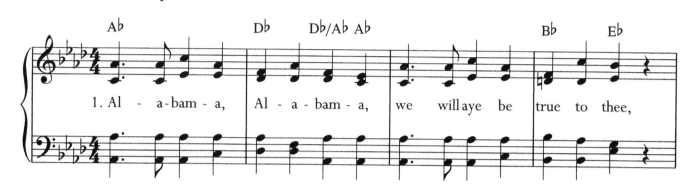

1. Al - a-bam - a, Al - a-bam - a, we will aye be true to thee,

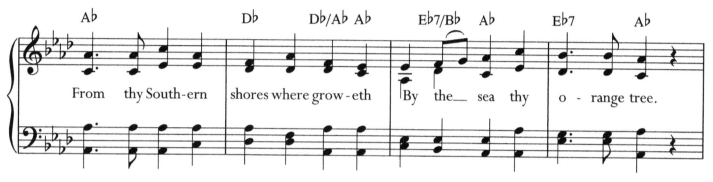

From thy South-ern shores where grow - eth By the__ sea thy o - range tree.

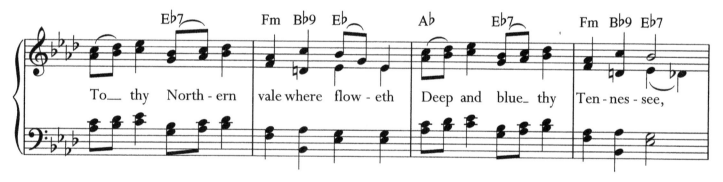

To__ thy North-ern vale where flow - eth Deep and blue_ thy Ten - nes - see,

Al - a-bam - a, Al - a-bam - a, we will_ aye be true to thee.

2. Broad thy stream whose name thou bearest,
Grand thy Bigbee rolls along
Fair thy Coosa-Tallapoosa,
Bold thy Warrior dark and strong.
Goodlier than the land that Moses
Climbed lone Nebb's Mount to see.
Alabama, Alabama, we will aye be true to thee.

3. Brave and pure thy men and women,
Better this than corn and wine,
Make us worthy, God in Heaven
Of this goodly land of Thine.
Hearts as open as thy doorways,
Liberal hands and spirits free,
Alabama, Alabama, we will aye be true to thee.

Away Rio
(Song of the Rio Grande)

American sea chanty

A - way _____ Ri - o, _____ We're

bound _____ a - way _____ on This ver - y day, Yes, we're

bound for the Ri - o Grande. _____

3. We've a jolly good ship and a jolly good crew
Away Rio.
A jolly good mate and a good skipper, too,
And we're bound for the Rio Grande.

4. Goodbye to Sally and goodbye to Sue
Away Rio.
And you who are listening, goodbye to you
And we're bound for the Rio Grande.

5. Heave with a will, and heave long and strong
Away Rio.
Sing the good chorus, for 'tis a good song
And we're bound for the Rio Grande.

6. The chains up and down now, the bosun did say
Away Rio.
Heave up the hause pipe, the anchor's a weigh,
And we're bound for the Rio Grande.

Carry Me Back to Old Virginny

(State Song Emeritus of Virginia)

Words and music by James A. Bland

Moderately slow

A tempo

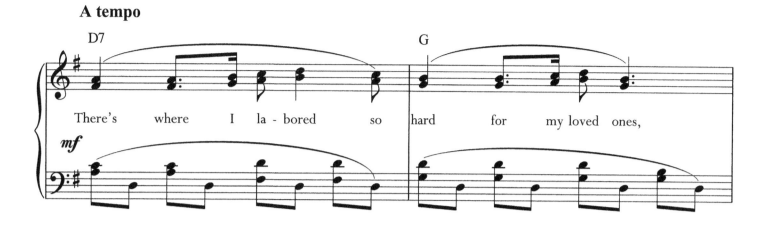

There's where I la-bored so hard for my loved ones,

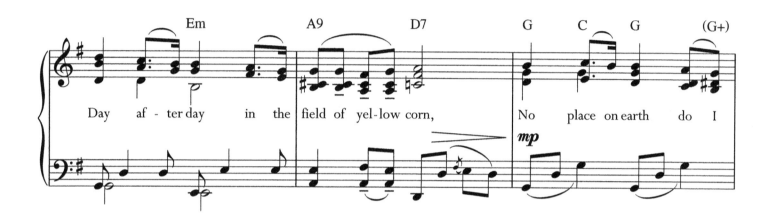

Day af-ter day in the field of yel-low corn, No place on earth do I

love more sin-cere-ly Than old Vir-gin-ny, The____ state where I was born.

2. Carry me back to old Virginny,
   There let me live till I wither and decay.
   Long by the old Dismal Swamp have I wandered,
   There's where this old dreamer's life will pass away.
   Momma and poppa have long gone before me;
   Soon we will meet on that bright and golden shore.
   There we'll be happy and free from all sorrow;
   There's where we'll meet and we'll never part no more.

Home on the Range

(State Song of Kansas)

American folk song

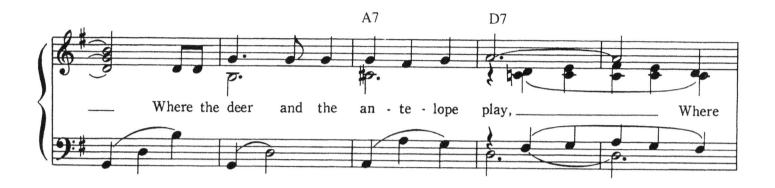

A7   D7

Where the deer   and the   an - te - lope   play, _____   Where

G   C   Cm

sel - dom   is   heard   a dis - cour - ag - ing   word,   And the

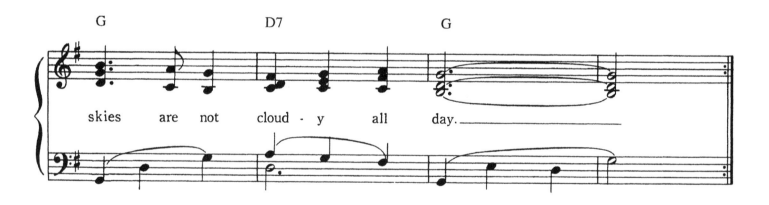

G   D7   G

skies   are   not   cloud - y   all   day. _____

3. Oh, give me a land where the bright diamond sand,
   Flows leisurely down the stream;
   Where the graceful, white swan goes gliding along,
   Like a maid in a heavenly dream.
   Refrain

4. How often at night when the heavens are bright,
   With the light of the glittering stars,
   Have I stood there amazed and asked as I gazed,
   If their glory exceeds that of ours.
   Refrain

Illinois
(State Song of Illinois)

Words and music by C.H. Chamberlain

Moderately

1. By the riv-ers gent-ly flow-ing, Il-li-nois, Il-li-nois, O'er thy

prair-ies ver-dant grow-ing, Il-li-nois, Il-li-nois, Comes an ech-o on the breeze, Rust-ling

through the leaf-y trees, And its mel-low tones are these,__ Il-li-

nois, Il-li-nois, And its mel-low tones are these,__ Il-li-nois.

2. From a wilderness of prairies, Illinois, Illinois,
Straight thy way and never varies, Illinois, Illinois,
Till upon the inland sea,
Stands thy great commercial tree,
Turning all the world to thee, Illinois, Illinois,
Turning all the world to thee, Illinois.

3. Not without thy wondrous story, Illinois, Illinois,
Can be writ the nation's glory, Illinois, Illinois;
On the record of thy years,
Abr'am Lincoln's name appears,
Grant and Logan, and our tears, Illinois, Illinois,
Grant and Logan, and our tears, Illinois.

Maryland! My Maryland!

(State Song of Maryland)

Words by James R. Randall
German carol "O Tannenbaum"

With a steady beat

3. I see no blush upon thy cheek,
Maryland! my Maryland!
Though thou wast ever bravely meek,
Maryland! my Maryland!
For life and death, for woe and weal,
Thy peerless chivalry revel,
And gird thy beauteous limbs with steel,
Maryland! my Maryland!

4. I hear the distant thunder hum,
Maryland! my Maryland!
The Old Line bugle, fife, and drum,
Maryland! my Maryland!
Come! to thine own heroic throng,
That stalks with Liberty along,
And ring thy dauntless slogan song,
Maryland! my Maryland!

Meet Me in St. Louis, Louis

Words by Andrew B. Sterline
Music by Kerry Mills

Brightly

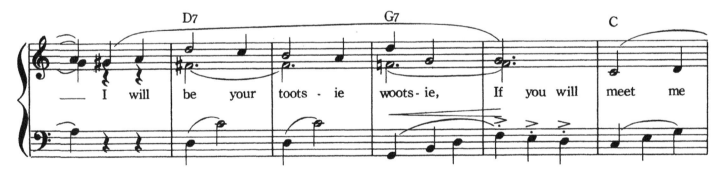

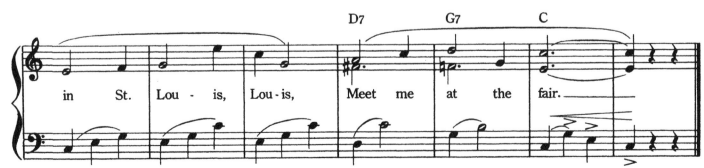

Michigan, My Michigan
(State Song of Michigan)

Words by Douglas Malloch
Music by W. Otto Miessner

With a steady beat

2. How fair the bosom of thy lakes,
Michigan, my Michigan;
What melody each river makes,
Michigan, my Michigan;
As to thy lakes thy rivers tend,
Thy exiled children to thee send
Devotion that shall never end,
Oh, Michigan, my Michigan.

3. Thou rich in wealth that makes a State,
Michigan, my Michigan;
Thou great in things that make us great,
Michigan, my Michigan;
Our loyal voices sound thy claim,
Upon the golden roll of Fame
Our loyal hands shall write the name
Of Michigan, my Michigan.

My Old Kentucky Home
(State Song of Kentucky)

Words and music by Stephen Foster

Moderately slow

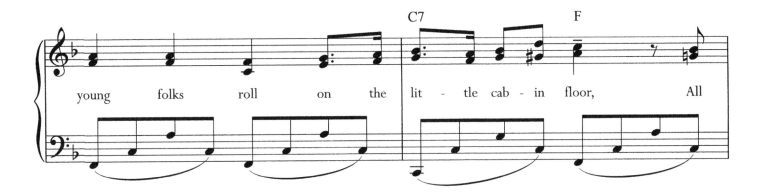

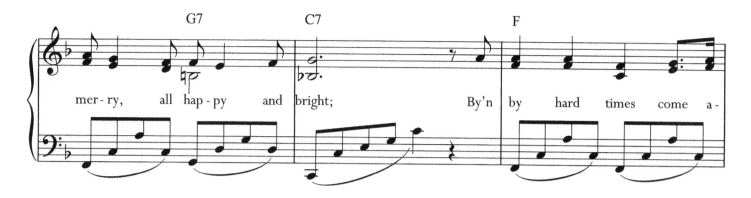

mer - ry, all hap - py and bright; By'n by hard times come a-

knock - ing at the door, Then my old Ken - tuck - y home, good night!

rit.

REFRAIN
A tempo

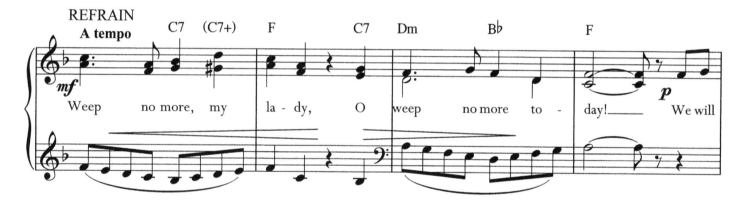

mf

Weep no more, my la - dy, O weep no more to - day!_____ We will

p

sing one song for the old Ken - tuck - y home, For the old Ken - tuck - y home, far a - way.

pp

New England, New England

Words by Anna M. Wells
Music by I. T. Stoddard

Moderately slow

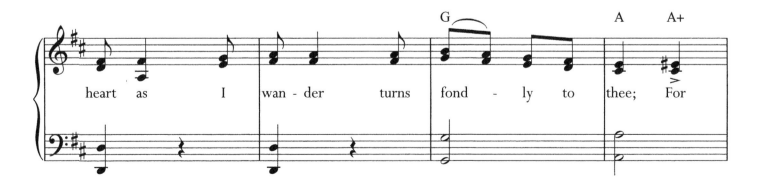

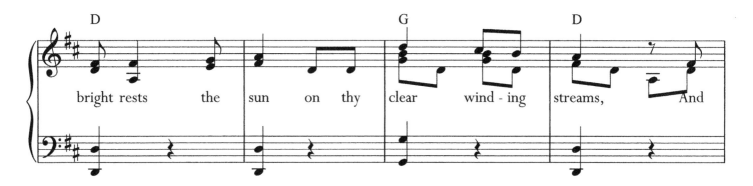

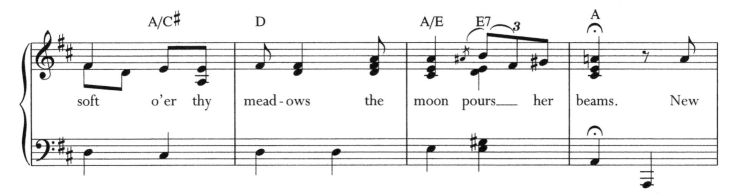

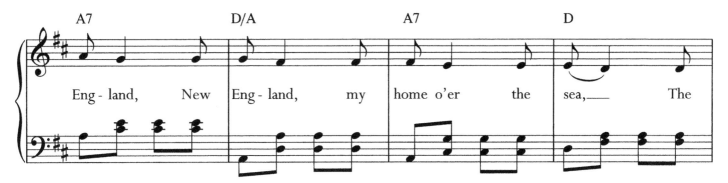

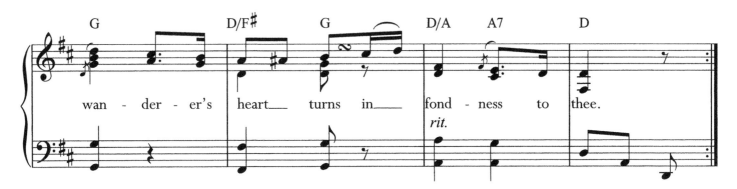

2. Thy breezes are healthful, and clear are thy rills,
And the harvest waves proudly and rich on thy hills;
Thy maidens are fair, and thy yeomen are strong,
And thy rivers run blithely thy valleys among.
New England, New England, my home o'er the sea,
The wanderer's heart turns in fondness to thee.

3. There's home in New England where dear ones of mine
Are thinking of me and the days of "Auld lang syne";
And blest be the hour when, my pilgrimage o'er,
I shall sit by that hearthstone and leave it no more.
New England, New England, my home o'er the sea,
My heart as I wander turns fondly to thee.

On the Banks of the Wabash
(State Song of Indiana)

Words and music by Paul Dresser

Moderato

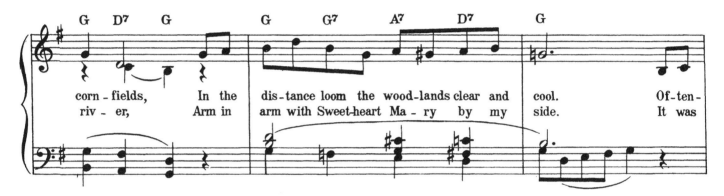

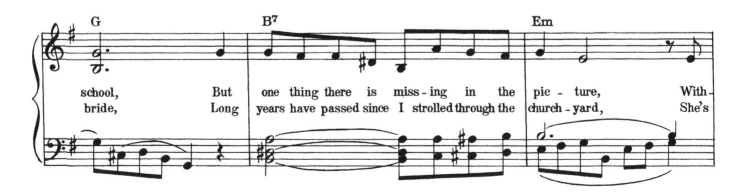

out her face it seems so in-com - plete.   I   long to see my moth-er   in the
sleep-ing there, my an - gel Ma-ry dear.   I   loved her but she thought I did-n't

door - way,   As she   stood there years a - go, her boy to   greet.   Oh, The
mean it,   Still I'd   give my fu - ture, were she on - ly there.

Chorus

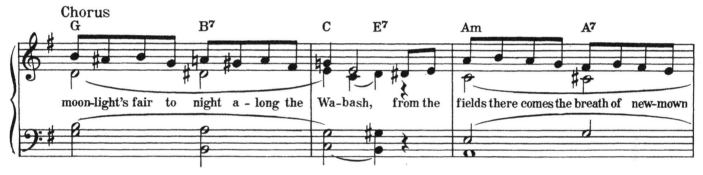

moon-light's fair to night a - long the Wa-bash,   from the   fields there comes the breath of new-mown

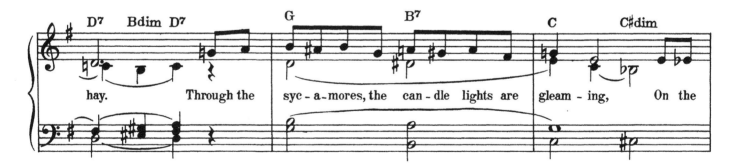

hay.   Through the   syc - a - mores, the can - dle lights are   gleam - ing,   On the

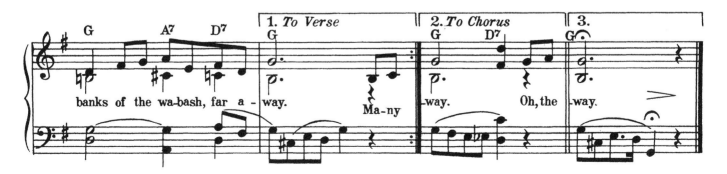

banks of the wa-bash, far a - way.   Ma-ny   way.   Oh, the   way.

On Wisconsin
(State Song of Wisconsin)

Words by Carl Beck
Music by W.T. Purdy

With spirit

Red River Valley

American cowboy song

3. I've been thinking a long time, my darling,
Of the sweet words you never would say,
Now, alas, must my fond hopes all vanish?
For they say you are going away.

4. They will bury me where you have wandered,
Near the hills where the daffodils grow,
When you're gone from the Red River Valley,
For I can't live without you I know.

She'll Be Comin' Round the Mountain

American folk song

2. She'll be drivin' six white horses when she comes, *etc.*

3. Oh, we'll all go out and meet her when she comes, *etc.*

4. We will kill the old red rooster when she comes, *etc.*

5. We will all have chicken and dumplings when she comes, *etc.*

The Sidewalks of New York

Charles B. Lawlor & James W. Blake

The Yellow Rose of Texas

American cowboy song

Moderately

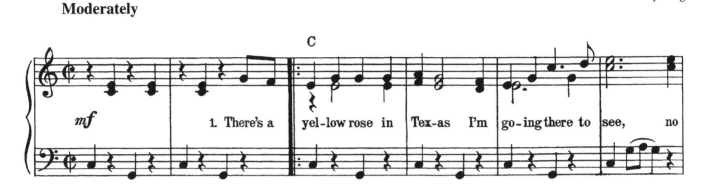

1. There's a yel-low rose in Tex-as I'm go-ing there to see, no

oth-er fel-low knows her, No-bod-y, on-ly me. She cried so, when I left her, it

like to broke her heart, and if we ev-er meet a-gain, we nev-er more shall part. She's the

REFRAIN

sweet-est rose of col-or, a fel-low ev-er knew, her eyes are bright as

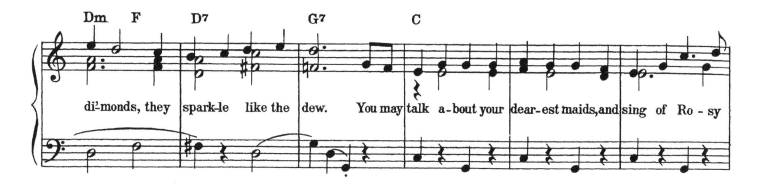

di²monds, they spark-le like the dew. You may talk a-bout your dear-est maids,and sing of Ro - sy

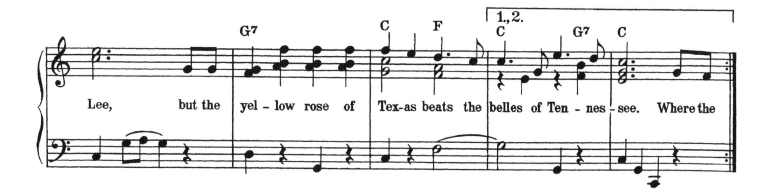

Lee, but the yel - low rose of Tex-as beats the belles of Ten - nes - see. Where the

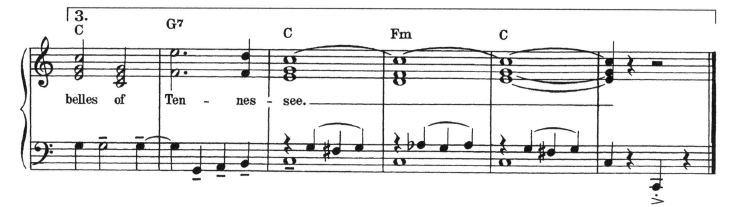

belles of Ten - nes - see. _____

2. Down beside the Rio Grande, the stars were shining bright,
   We walked along the river, on a quiet summer night.
   She said, "If you remember, we parted long ago,
   You promised to come back again, and never leave me so."

3. Oh, I'm going back to find her, my heart is full of woe,
   We'll sing the songs together, we sang so long ago.
   I'll pick the banjo gaily, and sing the songs of yore,
   The yellow rose of Texas, she'll be mine forevermore.

Way Down Upon the Swanee River

(State Song of Florida)

Words and music by Stephen Foster

Moderately slow

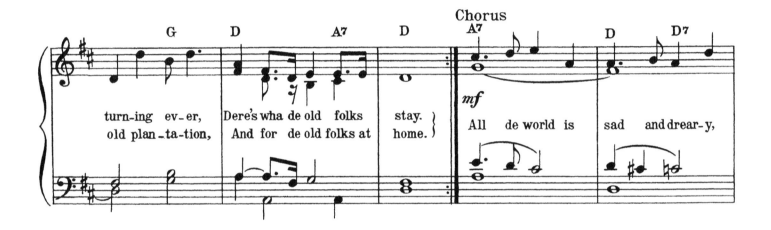

2. All 'round the little farm I wandered,
When I was young,
Then many happy days I squandered,
Many the songs I sung.
When I was playing with my brother,
Happy was I.
Oh! take me to my kind old mother,
There let me live and die.
Chorus

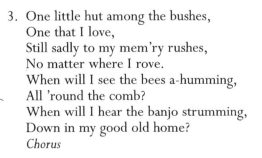

3. One little hut among the bushes,
One that I love,
Still sadly to my mem'ry rushes,
No matter where I rove.
When will I see the bees a-humming,
All 'round the comb?
When will I hear the banjo strumming,
Down in my good old home?
Chorus

FOR OUR SOLDIERS

The Army Hymn
(O Lord of Hosts)

Words by Oliver Wendell Holmes
Music by Henry Baker

Energetico

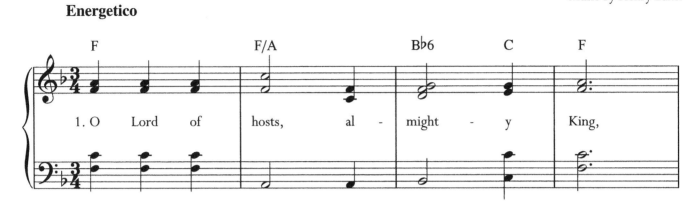

1. O Lord of hosts, al - might - y King,

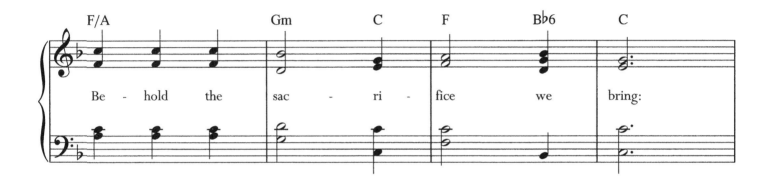

Be - hold the sac - ri - fice we bring:

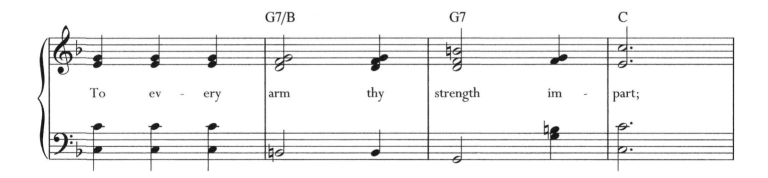

To ev - ery arm thy strength im - part;

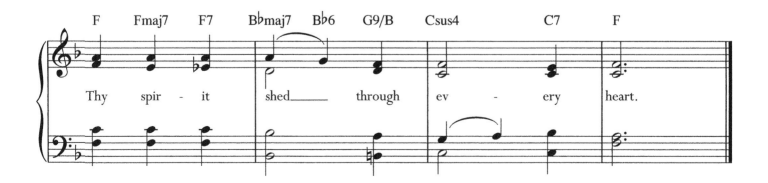

Thy spir - it shed_____ through ev - ery heart.

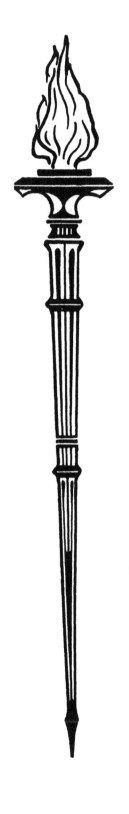

2. Wake in our breasts the living fires,
   The holy faith that warmed our sires;
   Thy hand hath made our nation free!
   To die for her is serving Thee.

3. Be Thou a pillar for to show
   The midnight snare, the silent foe;
   And when the battle thunders loud,
   Still guide us in its moving cloud.

4. God of all Nations; Sovereign Lord,
   In Thy dread name we draw the sword,
   We lift the starry flag on high,
   That fills with light our stormy sky.

5. From treason's rent, from murder's stain,
   Guard Thou its folds till peace shall reign,
   Till fort and field, till shore and sea
   Join our loud anthem: Praise to Thee!

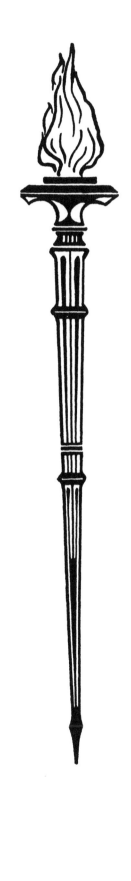

The Caissons Go Rolling Along

(The Army Anthem)

Music and words by Edmund L. Gruber

Energetico

O - ver hill, o - ver dale, as we hit the dust - y trail, And the cais - sons go

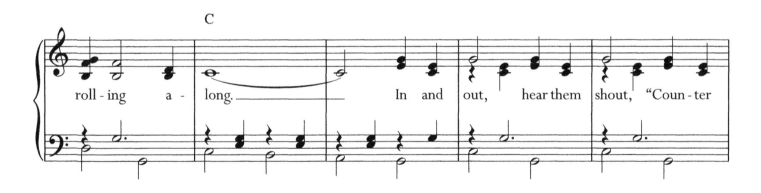

roll - ing a - long. In and out, hear them shout, "Coun - ter

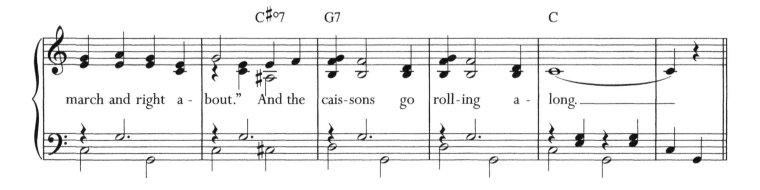

march and right a - bout." And the cais - sons go roll - ing a - long.

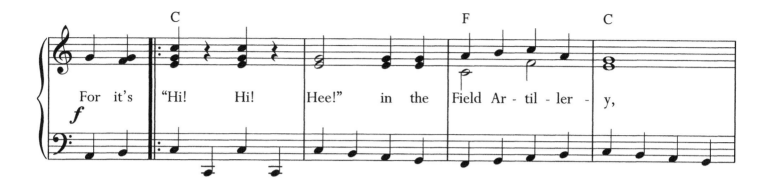

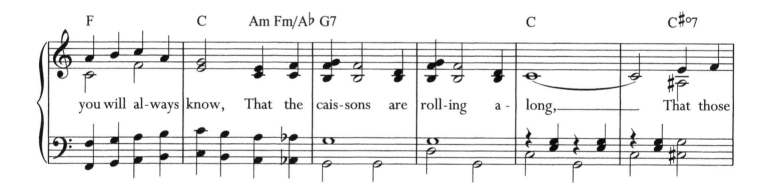

The Marines' Hymn
(From the Halls of Montezuma)

American anthem

Energetically

1. From the Halls of Mon - te - zu - ma To the

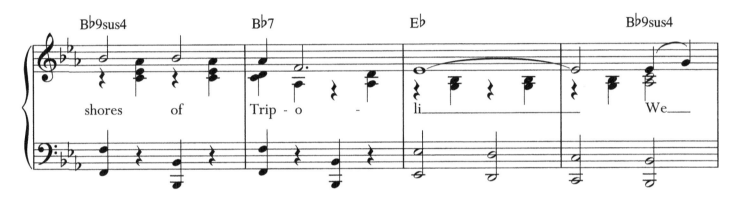

shores of Trip - o - li_____ We____

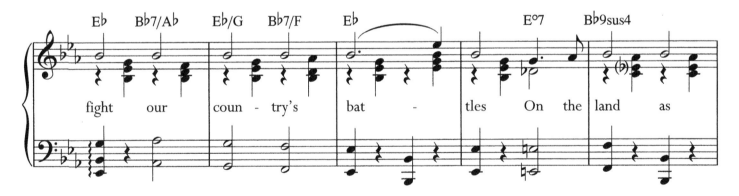

fight our coun - try's bat - tles On the land as

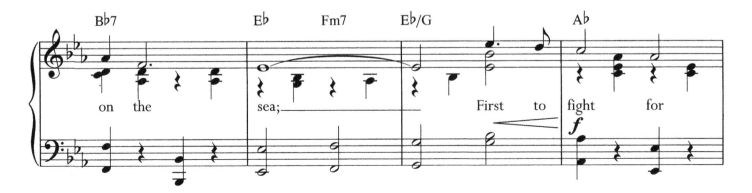

on the sea;_____ First to fight for

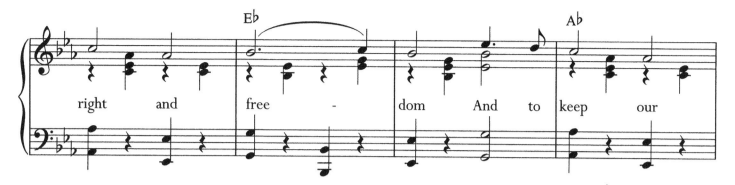

right and free - dom And to keep our

hon - or clean; We are proud to claim the

mf

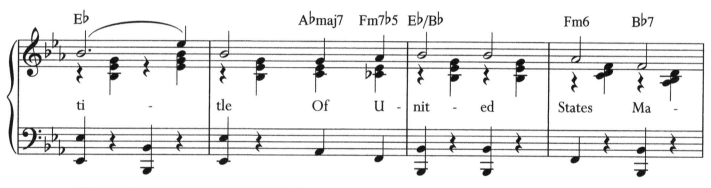

ti - tle Of U - nit - ed States Ma -

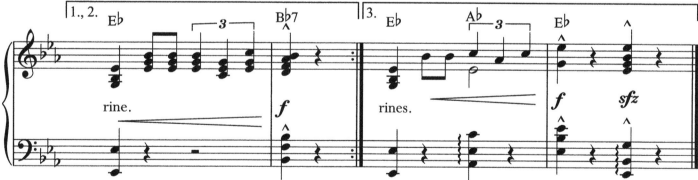

1., 2. rine. *f*

3. rines. *f* *sfz*

2. Our flag's unfurled to every breeze,
From dawn to setting sun.
We have fouhgt in every clime and place,
Where we could take a gun.
In the snow of far-off Northern lands,
And in sunny Tropic scenes,
You will find us always on the job,
The United States Marines.

3. Here's health to you and to our Corps,
Which we are proud to serve.
In many a strife we've fought for life,
And never lost our nerve.
If the Army and the Navy,
Ever look on Heaven's scenes,
They will find the streets are guarded
By United States Marines.

Over There

Words and music by George M. Cohan

With a steady beat

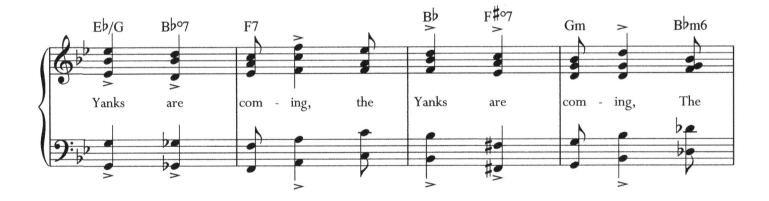

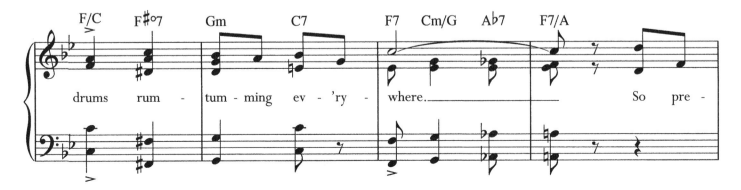

pare, _____ say a prayer, _____ Send the

word, send the word to be - ware. _____ We'll be

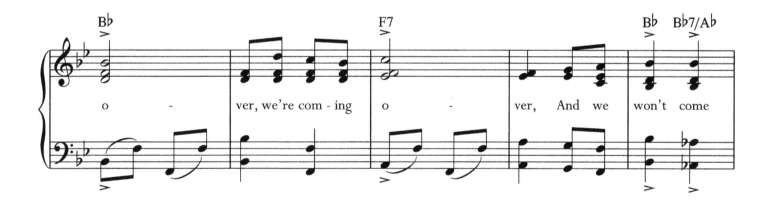

o - ver, we're com - ing o - ver, And we won't come

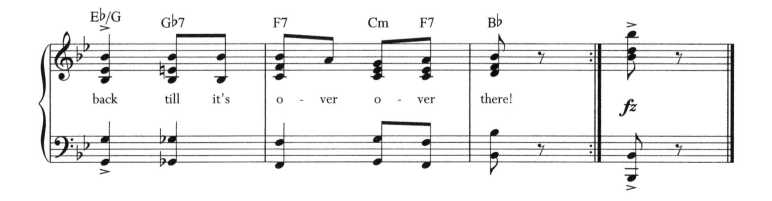

back till it's o - ver o - ver there!

Tenting Tonight

Words and music by William Kittridge

Moderately slow

1. We're — tent-ing to-night on the old camp-ground, Give us a song to cheer our
4. We've been fight-ing to-day on the old camp-ground, Man-y are ly-ing near, —

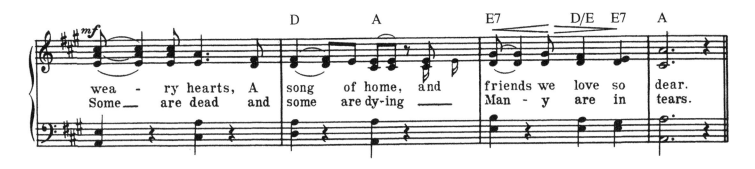

wea - ry hearts, A song of home, and friends we love so dear.
Some — are dead and some are dy-ing — Man-y are in tears.

Man-y are the hearts that are wea-ry to-night, Wish-ing for the war to end;

Man-y are the hearts look-ing for the right, To see the dawn of peace. Tent-ing to-night,
Dy-ing to-night,

Tent-ing to-night,
Dy-ing to-night,

1. tent-ing on the old camp ground.

2. Dy-ing on the old camp ground.

Tramp, Tramp, Tramp

Words and music by George F. Root

Yankee Doodle

American marching song

Brightly

1. Fath'r and I went down to camp, A - long with Cap - tain Good - 'in, And

there we saw the men and boys as thick as has - ty pud - din'.

REFRAIN

Yan - kee Doo - dle keep it up, Yan - kee Doo - dle Dan - dy,

Mind the mus - ic and the step, And with the girls be hand - y.

2. And there we saw a thousand men,
   As rich as Squire David;
   And what they wasted ev'ry day,
   I wish it could be savèd.
   Refrain

3. And there was Captain Washington,
   Upon a slapping stallion,
   A-giving orders to his men;
   I guess there was a million.
   Refrain

4. And there I saw a swamping gun,
   Large as a log of maple,
   Upon a mighty little cart;
   A load for father's cattle.
   Refrain

5. And every time they fired it off,
   It took a horn of powder;
   It made a noise like father's gun,
   Only a nation louder.
   Refrain

6. And there I saw a little keg,
   Its head all made of leather,
   They knocked upon't with little sticks
   To call the folks together.
   Refrain

7. The troopers then would gallop up
   And fire right in our faces;
   It scared me almost half to death
   To see them run such races.
   Refrain

8. But I can't tell you half I saw,
   They kept up such a smother;
   So I took my hat off, made a bow,
   And scampered home to mother.
   Refrain

9. Yankee Doodle went to town,
   A-riding on a pony;
   Stuck a feather in his cap,
   And called it macaroni.

Yankee Doodle Dandy

Words and music by George M. Cohan

Moderately

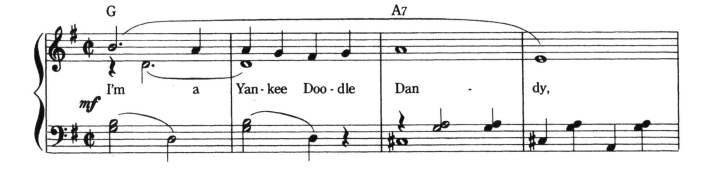

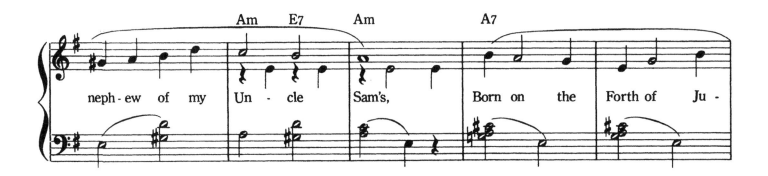

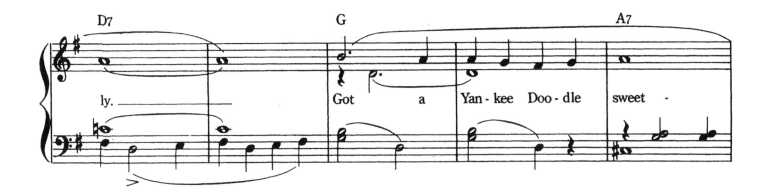

heart, She's my Yan - kee Doo - dle joy. ____

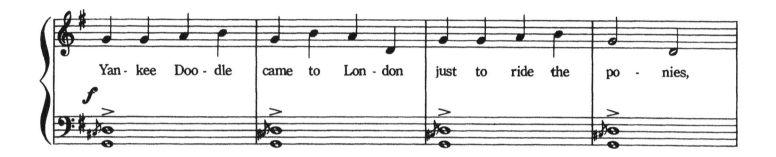

Yan - kee Doo - dle came to Lon - don just to ride the po - nies,

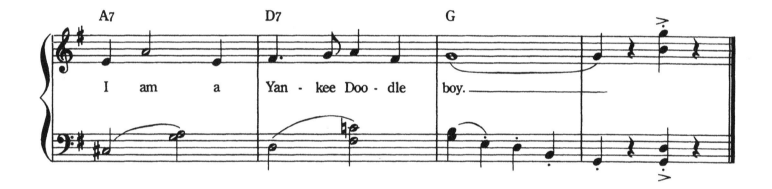

I am a Yan - kee Doo - dle boy. ____

You're in the Army Now

American marching song

With a steady beat

mf
You're in the Arm - y now,_____ You're not__ be-hind the plow;_____ You'll

nev - er get rich A - dig-ging a ditch, You're in the Arm - y now._____ You're

in the Arm - y now,_____ You're in the Arm - y now,_____ You'll

nev - er get rich On the sal - a - ry which You get in the Arm - y now._____

FOR OUR SAILORS
AND FLYERS

The Air Force Hymn
(Lord, Guard and Guide the Men Who Fly)

Words by Mary C.D. Hamilton
Music by Henry Baker

Moderately

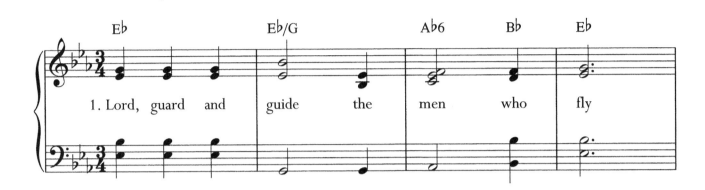

1. Lord, guard and guide the men who fly

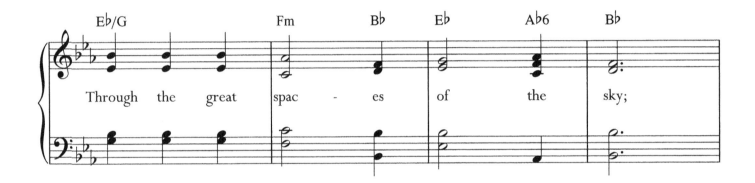

Through the great spac - es of the sky;

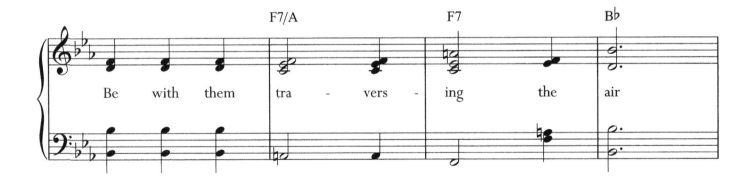

Be with them tra - vers - ing the air

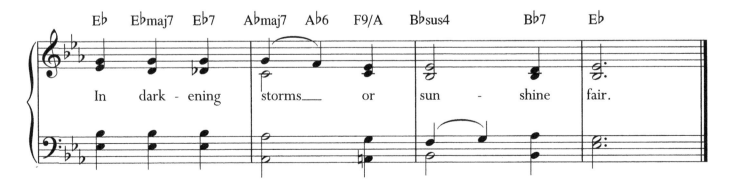

In dark - ening storms___ or sun - shine fair.

2. You who support with tender might
The balanced birds in all their flight,
Lord of the tempered winds, be near,
That, having you, they know no fear.

3. Control their minds with instinct fit
Whene'er, adventuring, they quit
The firm security of land;
Grant steadfast eye and skillful hand.

4. Aloft in solitudes of space,
Uphold them with your saving grace.
O God, protect the men who fly
Through lonely ways beneath the sky.

Anchors Aweigh

Words by Alfred Hart Miles and R. Lovell
Music by Charles A. Zimmerman

Energetico

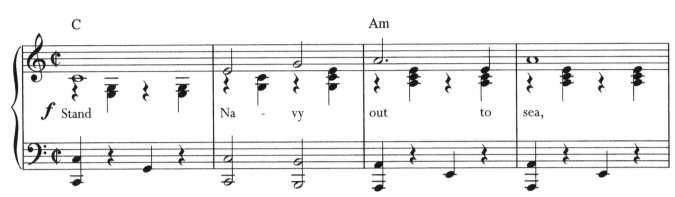

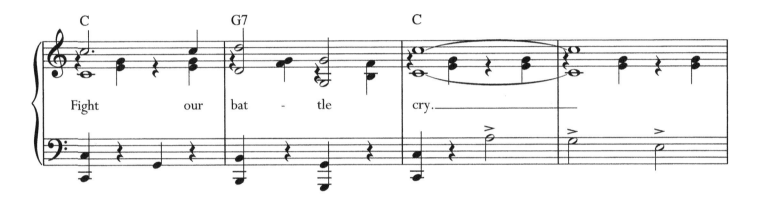

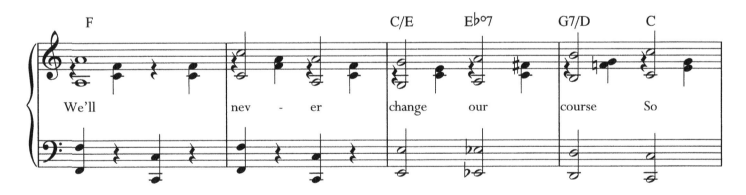

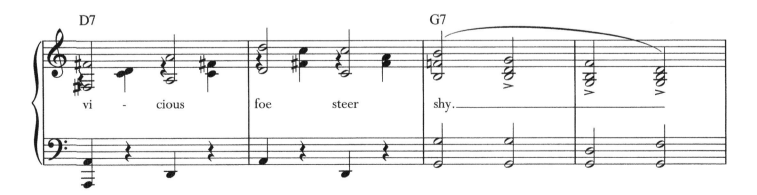

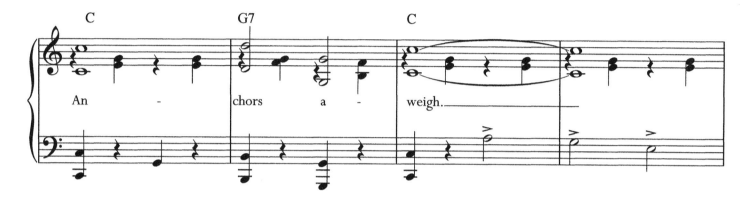

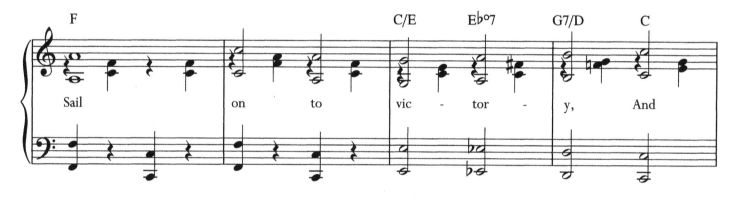

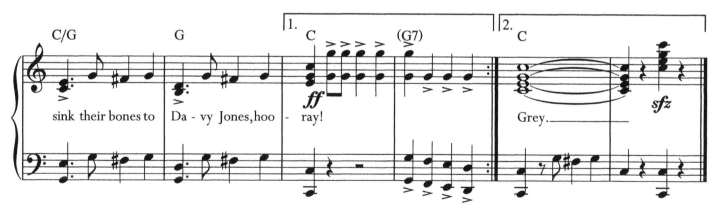

College Version

1. Anchors aweigh, my boys,
   Anchors aweigh.
   Farewell to college joys,
   We sail at break of day.
   Through our last night on shore,
   Drink to the foam;
   Until we meet once more,
   Here's wishing you a happy voyage home.

2. Stand, Navy, down the field,
   Sail to the sky.
   We'll never change our course,
   So, Army, you steer shy.
   Roll up the score, Navy,
   Anchors aweigh.
   Sail, Navy, down the field,
   And sink the Army, sink the Army Grey.

Columbia, the Gem of the Ocean

Words and music by David T. Shaw and Thomas A. Becket

With a steady beat

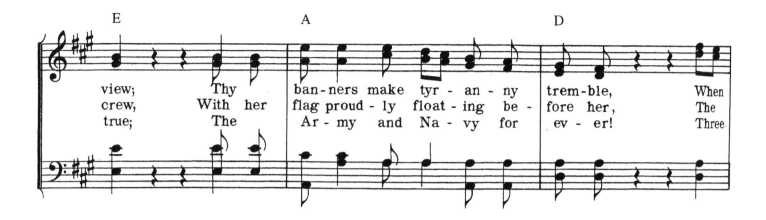

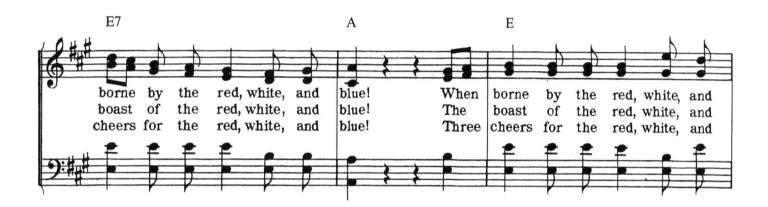

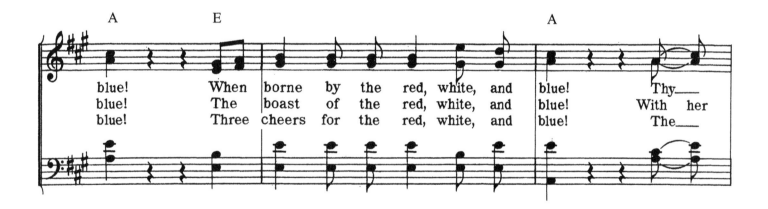

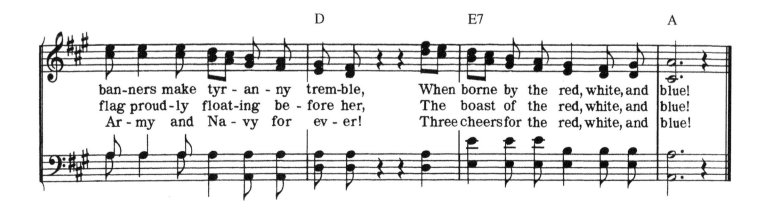

Blow the Man Down

English-American sea chantey

2. As I was a-walkin' down Paradise Street,
   To me way, hey, blow the man down,
   A pretty young damsel I chanced for to meet,
   Give me some time to blow the man down.

3. And as we were going she said unto me,
   To me way, hey, blow the man down,
   "There's a spanking full-rigger just ready for sea."
   Give me some time to blow the man down.

4. As soon as that packet was out on the sea,
   To me way, hey, blow thte man down,
   'Twas devilish hard treatment of every degree,
   Give me some time to blow the man down.

5. So I give you fair warning before we belay,
   To me way, hey, blow the man down,
   Don't ever take heed of what pretty girls say,
   Give me some time to blow the man down.

Jesus, Savior, Pilot Me

(Navy Prayer)

Words by Edward Hopper
Music by John E. Gould

Moderately

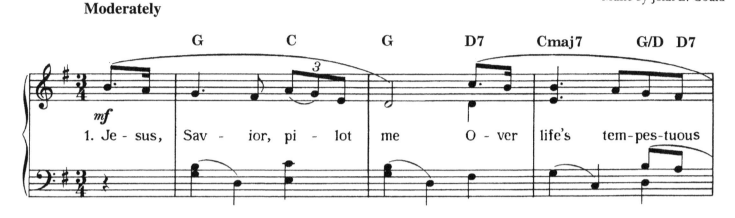

mf
1. Je - sus, Sav - ior, pi - lot me O - ver life's tem-pes-tuous

sea; Un-known waves be-fore me roll, Hid - ing rock and treach-erous

shoal; Chart and com - pass came from Thee: Je - sus, Sav - ior, pi - lot me.

2. As a mother stills her child,
Thou canst hush the ocean wild,
Boisterous waves obey Thy will
When Thou sayest to them, "Be still!"
Wondrous Sovereign of the sea,
Jesus, Savior, pilot me.

3. When at last I near the shore,
And the fearful breakers roar
'Twixt me and the peaceful rest,
Then, while leaning on Thy breast,
May I hear Thee say to me,
"Fear not, I will pilot thee."

A Life on the Ocean Wave

Words by Epes Sargent
Music by Henry Russell

Energetically

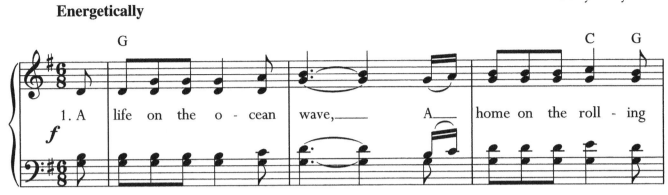

1. A life on the o - cean wave,___ A___ home on the roll - ing

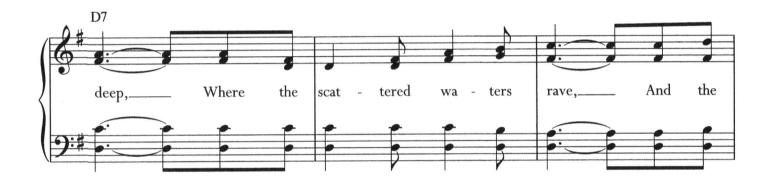

deep,___ Where the scat - tered wa - ters rave,___ And the

winds their rev - els keep! Like an ea - gle caged, I

pine,___ On this dull, un - chang - ing shore;___ Oh,

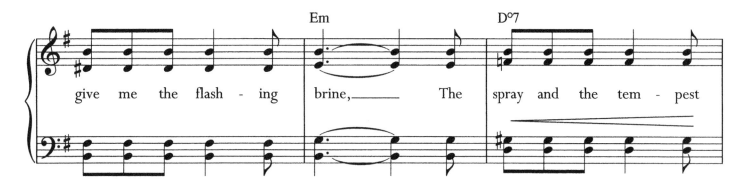

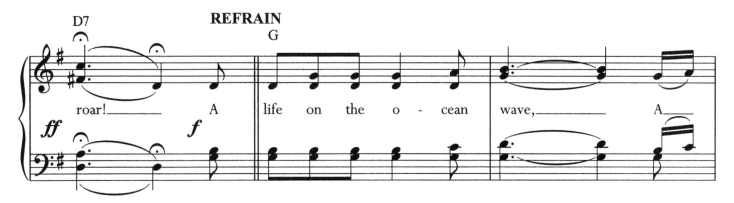

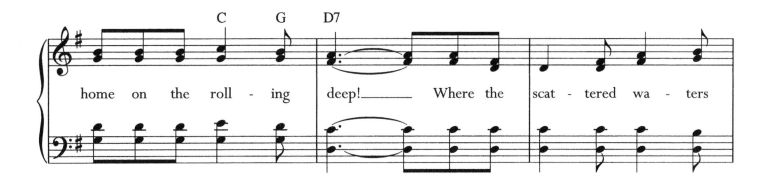

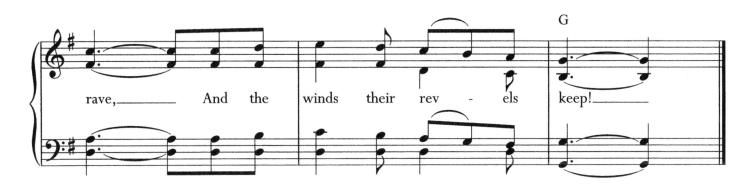

2. Once more on the deck I stand
Of my own swift-gliding craft;
Set sail! farewell to the land,
The gale follows far abaft:
We shoot through the sparkling foam,
Like an ocean bird set free;
Like the ocean bird, our home
We'll find far out on the sea!
Refrain

3. The land is no longer in view,
The clouds have begun to frown,
But with a stout vessel and crew,
We'll say, let the storm come down!
And the song of our heart shall be,
While the winds and the waters rave,
A life on the heaving sea,
A home on the bounding wave!
Refrain

My Bonnie Lies Over the Ocean

Scottish folk song

Moderately

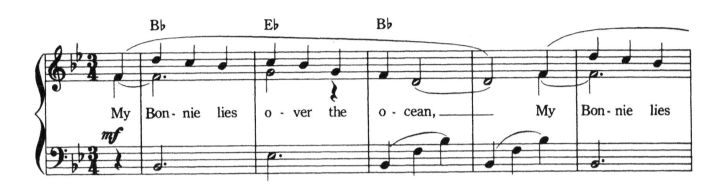

back, bring back, Oh bring back my Bon-nie to me.

2. The heather is blooming around me,
The blossoms of spring now appear,
The meadows with green'ry surround me,
Oh Bonnie, I wish you were here.
Refrain

3. Oh blow ye winds over the ocean,
Oh blow ye winds over the sea,
Oh blow ye winds over the ocean,
And bring back my Bonnie to me.
Refrain

4. The winds will blow over the ocean,
The winds will blow over the sea,
The winds will blow over the ocean,
And bring back my Bonnie to me.
Refrain

The Navy Hymn
(Eternal Father, Strong to Save)

Words by William Whiting
Music by John B. Dykes

Moderately slow

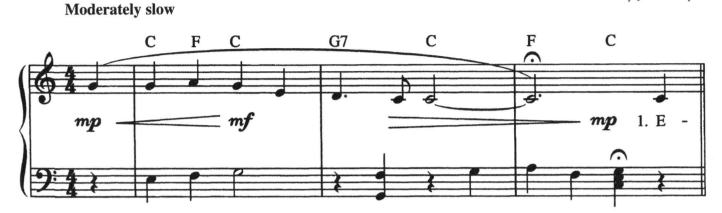

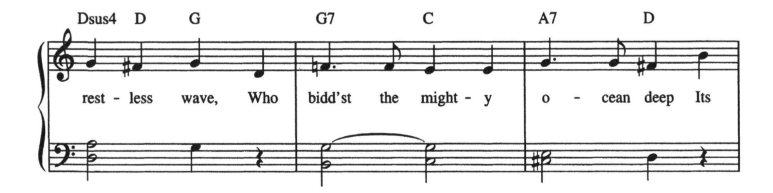

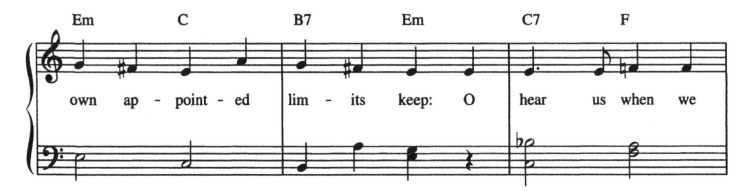

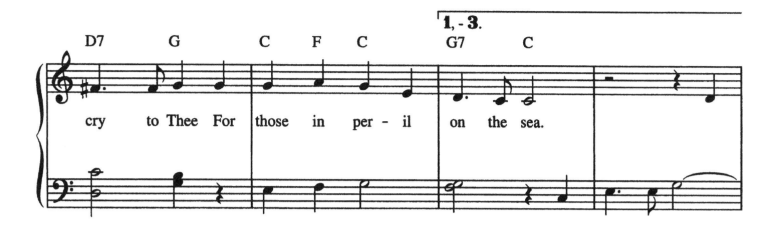

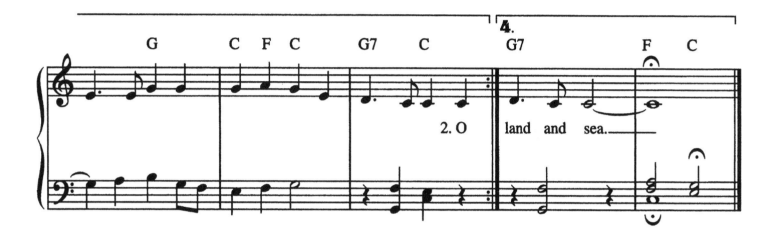

2. O Savior whose almighty word
   The winds and waves submissive heard,
   Who walkedst on the foaming deep
   And calm amid its rage did sleep:
   O hear us when we cry to Thee
   For those in peril on the sea.

3. O sacred Spirit, who didst brood
   Upon the waters dark and rude,
   And bid their angry tumult cease,
   And give, for wild confusion, peace:
   O hear us when we cry to Thee
   For those in peril on the sea.

4. O Trinity of love and power,
   Our brethren shield in danger's hour:
   From rock and tempest, fire and foe,
   Protect them wheresoe'er they go;
   And over let there rise to Thee
   Glad hymns of praise from land and sea.

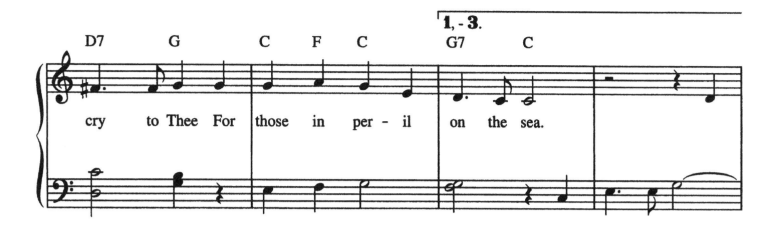

Sailing, Sailing

Words and music by Godfrey Marks

Moderately fast

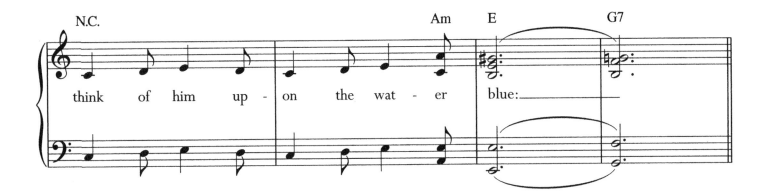

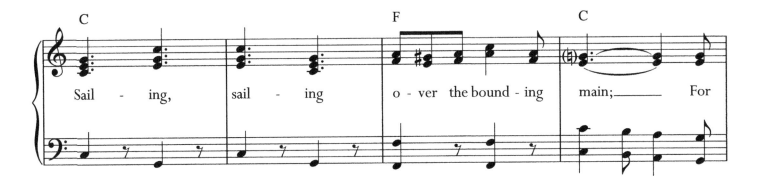

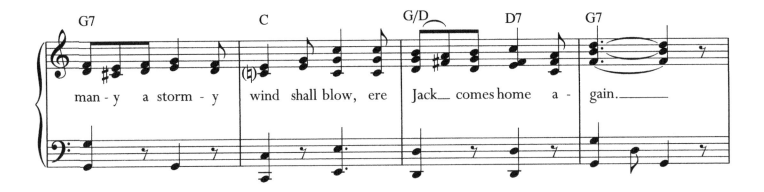

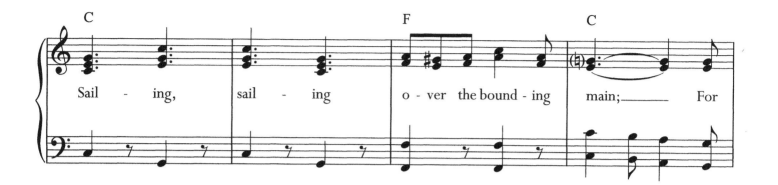

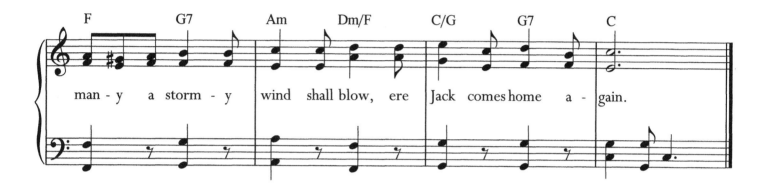

Sail - ing, sail - ing o - ver the bound - ing main;_____ For man - y a storm - y wind shall blow, ere Jack comes home a - gain.

The Spacious Firmament on High
(Flyer's Hymn)

Words by Joseph Addison
Music by Franz Joseph Haydn
from *The Creation*

Majestically

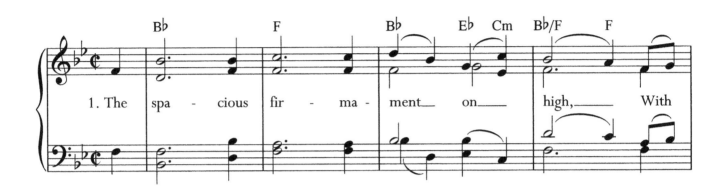

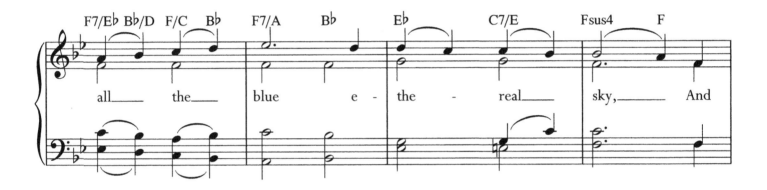

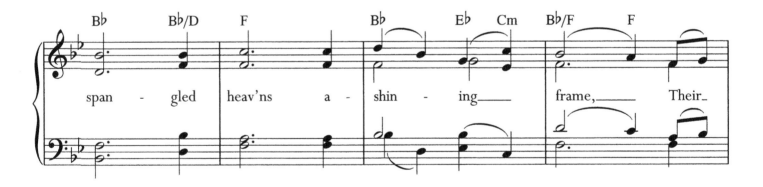

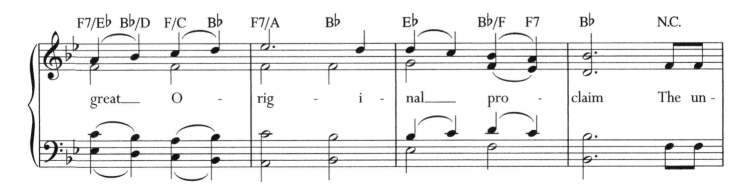

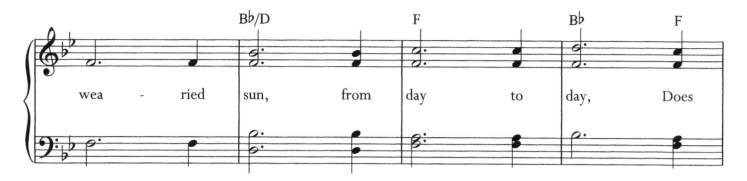

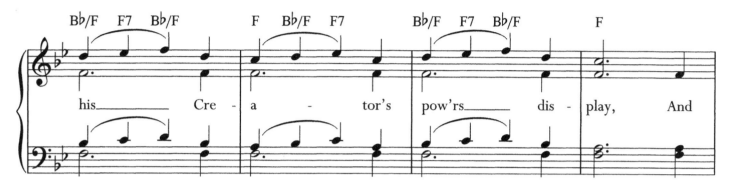

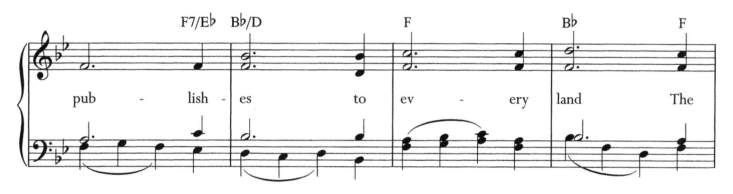

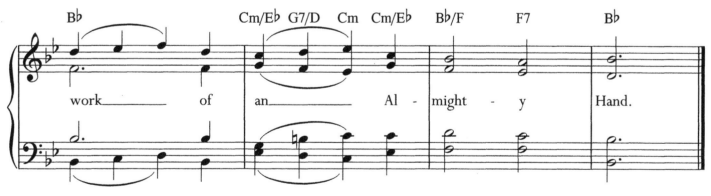

2. Soon as the evening shades prevail,
   The moon takes up the wondrous tale,
   And nightly to the list'ning earth,
   Repeats the story of her birth;
   While all the stars that round her burn,
   And all the planets in their turn,
   Confirm the tidings as they roll,
   And spread the truth from pole to pole.

3. What though in solemn silence all
   Move round the dark terrestrial ball?
   What though no real voice nor sound
   Amid the radiant orbs be found?
   In reason's ear they all rejoice,
   And utter forth a glorious voice,
   Forever singing as they shine,
   "The Hand that made us is Divine."

ON THE HOME FRONT

God Be with You till We Meet Again

Words by Rev. J.E. Rankin, D.D.
Music by W.G. Tomer

2. God be with you till we meet again,
When life's perils thick confound you,
Put His arms unfailing round you,
God be with you till we meet again.
Refrain

3. God be with you till we meet again,
Keep love's banner floating o'er you;
Smite death's threat'ning wave before you,
God be with you till we meet again.
Refrain

The Girl I Left Behind Me

Words by Samuel Lover
Irish air

Moderately

1. The hour was sad, I left the maid, A lin-g'ring fare-well tak-ing, Her sighs and tears my steps de-layed, I thought my heart was break-ing; In hur-ried words her name I blest, I breathed the vows that bind me, And to my heart in an-guish pressed The girl I left be-hind me.

2. Then to the East we bore a-way To win a name in sto-ry, And then warm downs the sun of day, There dawned our sun of glo-ry, Both blazed in noon on Al-ma's height, Where in the post as-signed me, I shared the glo-ry of that fight, Sweet girl I left be-hind me.

3. Full many a name our banners bore,
Of former deeds of daring,
But they were of the days of yore,
In which we had no sharing;
But now, our laurels freshly won,
With the old ones shall entwined be,
Still worthy of our sires each son,
Sweet girl I left behind me.

4. The hope of final victory,
Within my bosom burning,
Is mingling with sweet thoughts of thee,
And of my fond returning;
But should I ne'er return again,
Still worth your love you'll find me,
Dishonor's breath shall never stain,
The name I'll leave behind me.

Home Again from a Foreign Shore

Words and music by Marshall S. Pike

Moderately slow

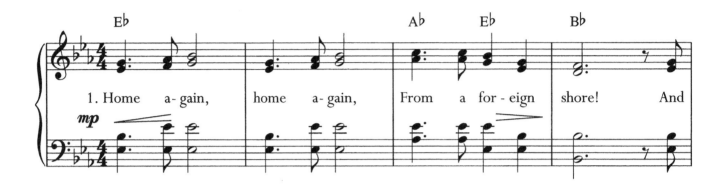

1. Home a-gain, home a-gain, From a for-eign shore! And

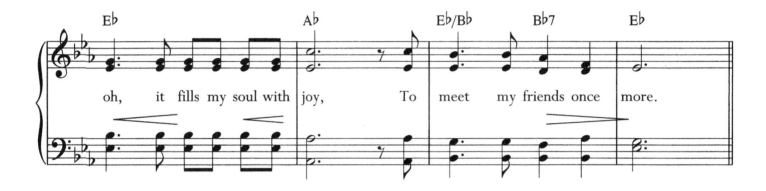

oh, it fills my soul with joy, To meet my friends once more.

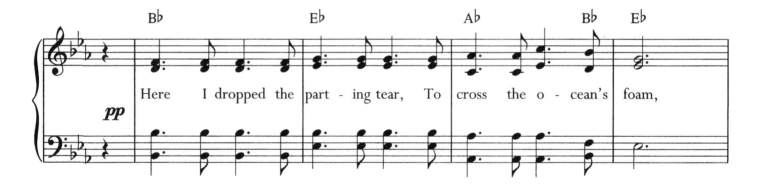

Here I dropped the part-ing tear, To cross the o-cean's foam,

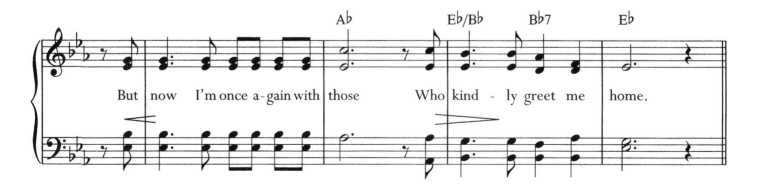

But now I'm once a-gain with those Who kind-ly greet me home.

REFRAIN

Home a-gain, home a-gain, From a for-eign shore! And

oh, it fills my soul with joy, To meet my friends once more.

2. Happy hearts, happy hearts,
   With mine have laughed in glee,
   And oh, the friends I loved in youth,
   Seem happier to me;
   And if my guide should be the fate,
   Which bids me longer roam,
   But death alone can break the tie
   That binds my heart to home.
   Refrain

3. Music sweet, music soft,
   Lingers round the place,
   And oh, I feel the childhood charm
   That time cannot efface.
   Then give me but my homestead roof,
   I'll ask no palace dome,
   For I can live a happy life
   With those I love at home.
   Refrain

Home, Sweet Home

Words and music by Henry R. Bishop

Slowly

'Mid___ pleas - ures and pal - a - ces,___ though___ we may

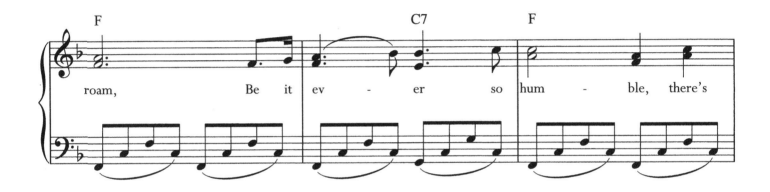

roam, Be it ev - er so hum - ble, there's

no___ place like home. A charm___ from the

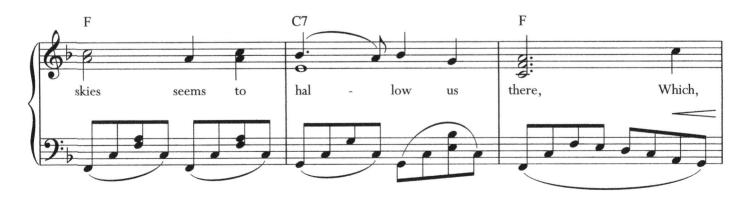

skies seems to hal - low us there, Which,

2. I gaze on the moon as I tread the drear wild,
   And feel that my mother now thinks of her child,
   As she looks on that moon from our own cottage door,
   Through the woodbine whose fragrance shall cheer me no more.
   Refrain

3. An exile from home, splendor dazzles in vain;
   Oh, give me a lowly thatched cottage again;
   The birds singing gaily, that came at my call,
   Give me them, and that peace of mind, dearer than all.
   Refrain

Keep the Home Fires Burning

Words by Lea Guilbert Ford
Music by Ivor Novello

Lento

They were sum-moned from the hill - side, They were called in from the

glen, And the coun - try found them read - y at the stir - ring call for

D
men._____ Let no tears add to their hard-ships, As the

sol - diers pass a - long, And al- though your heart is break-ing, Make it

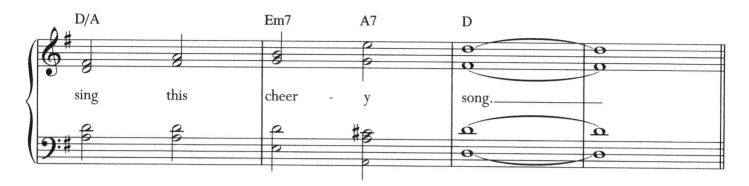

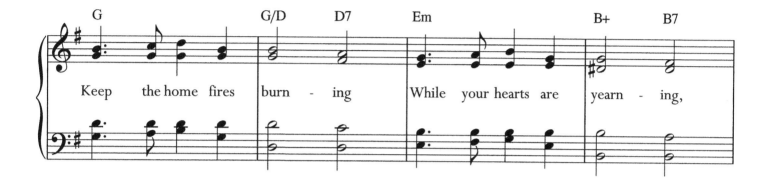

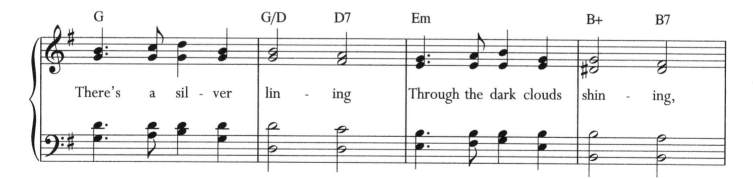

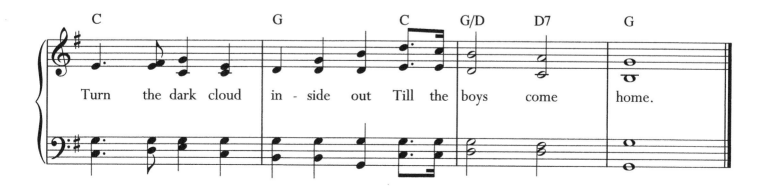

She Wore a Yellow Ribbon

Words and music by George A. Norton

With a steady beat

'Round her neck she wore a yel-low rib-bon, She wore it in the win-ter and the sum-mer so they say. If you ask her, "Why the dec - o - ra- tion?" She'll say, "It's for my sweet-heart who is far, far a - way." Far a - way, far a- way, If she is milk - in' cows or mow - in' hay;

'Round her neck she wore a yel-low rib-bon, She

wore it for her sweet-heart who is | far, far a-way. | far, far a-way!

Sweet and Low

Words by Alfred, Lord Tennyson
Music by Joseph Barnby

Gently

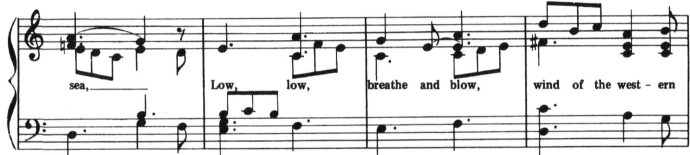

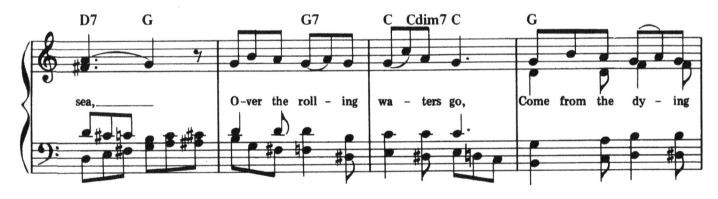

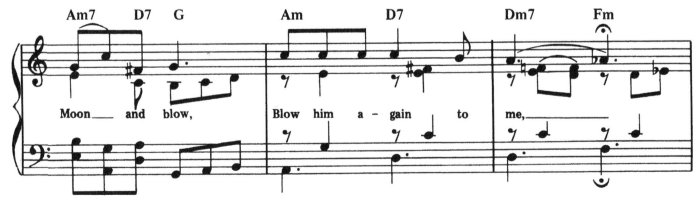

While my lit – tle one, while my pret-ty one, sleeps.

4. Sleep and rest, sleep and rest,
Father will come to thee soon;
Rest, rest on mother's breast,
Father will come to thee soon;
Father will come to his babe in the nest,
Silver sails all out of the west,
Under the silver moon,
Sleep, my little one, sleep, my pretty one, sleep.

The Soldier's Farewell

Words and music by Johanna Kinkel

Moderately slow

1. Ah, love, how can I leave thee? The sad thought deep doth grieve me; But know, what-e'er be-falls me, I go where hon-or calls me. Fare-

cresc.

REFRAIN

tranquillo e molto espress.

well, fare-well, my own true love! Fare-well, fare-well, my own true love!

2. Ne'er more may I behold thee,
   Or to my heart enfold thee;
   In work array appearing,
   The foe's stern hosts are nearing.
   Refrain

3. I think of thee with longing;
   Think thou, when tears are thronging,
   That with my last faint sighing
   I'll whisper soft, while dying,
   Refrain

When Johnny Comes Marching Home

Words and music by Patrick S. Gilmore

2. The old church bell will peal with joy,
Hurrah, hurrah!
To welcome home our darling boy,
Hurrah, hurrah!
The village lads and lassies say,
With roses they will strew the way,
And we'll all feel gay
When Johnny comes marching home.

3. Get ready for the jubilee,
Hurrah, hurrah!
We'll give the hero three times three,
Hurrah, hurrah!
The laurel wreath is ready now,
To place upon his loyal brow,
And we'll all feel gay
When Johnny comes marching home.

FOR THE FALLEN

Amazing Grace

Words by John Newton
Scottish air

Freely

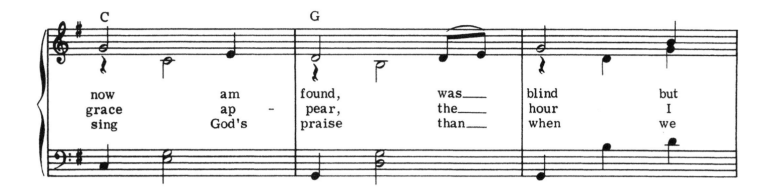

now   am   found,   was___   blind   but
grace   ap - pear,   the___   hour   I
sing   God's praise   than___   when   we

now   can   see.___   2. 'Twas
first   be - lieved.___   3. When
first   be - gun.___

4. Through many dangers, toils, and snares,
   I have already come.
   'Tis grace that brought me safe thus far,
   And grace will lead me home.

5. How sweet the name of Jesus sounds,
   In a believer's ear.
   It soothes his sorrow, heals his wounds,
   And drives away his fear.

6. Amazing grace, how sweet the sound
   That saved a wretch like me.
   I once was lost, but now am found,
   Was blind but now can see.

Cherished Names

Words by Samuel Francis Smith
Music by L.B. Marshall

Quietly

1. We wreathe with flowers the peace-ful graves, Where low our fall-en com-rades sleep; While sun-beams smile, and verdure waves, And dews of eve-ning o'er them weep.

2. Honored and loved, each cherished name;
In vain, ye have not lived nor died;
A grateful country keeps your fame,
A sacred trust—her joy and pride.

3. God bless the land ye nobly saved,
Where'er your blood has left its stain,
Where'er your conquering banner waved,
May peace prevail and freedom reign.

Comrades, Sleep

Words by Samuel Francis Smith
Music by L.B. Marshall

Tenderly

1. Sleep, com - rades, in your glo - ry! Sweet be your hon - ored rest;

Thou - sands shall tell the sto - ry How ye, your high be - hest,

Brave - ly in love ful - fill - ing, Gave up your lives, to be

A sac - ri - fice most will - ing, The seal of lib - er - ty.

2. Oft as the springtime, breathing
   Sweet odors from fair flow'rs,
   With dewy pearls, comes wreathing
   Our bright and peaceful bow'rs,
   We bring the first and fairest,
   In honor to the brave,
   The choicest and the rarest,
   To deck the soldier's grave.

3. God of our country, o'er us
   Thy shield of glory spread!
   Go Thou in love before us;
   Direct the paths we tread.
   Faithful in ev'ry duty,
   To us Thy grace be giv'n,
   And then, the crowning beauty
   Of fadeless wreaths in heav'n.

Danny Boy

Irish air

With feeling

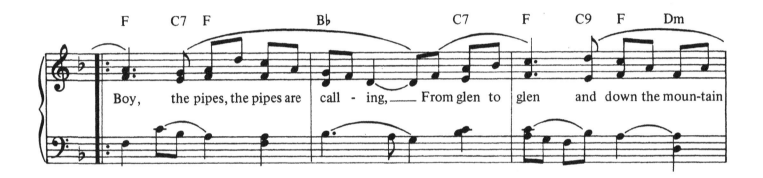

Boy, the pipes, the pipes are call - ing, ___ From glen to glen and down the moun-tain

side, ___ The sum-mer's gone and all the ros - es fall - ing, ___ It's you it's

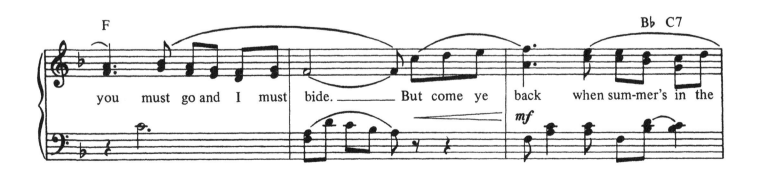

you must go and I must bide. ___ But come ye back when sum-mer's in the

mea - dow, ___ Or when the val - ley's hushed and white with snow, ___ It's I'll be

here in sun-shine or in sha - dow, __ Oh, Dan-ny Boy, oh Dan-ny Boy, I love you

so. ___ 2. And if you sleep in peace un-til you come to me. ___

2. And if you come when all the flowers are dying,
   And I am dead, as dead I well may be,
   You'll come and find the place where I am lying,
   And kneel and say an 'Ave' there for me.
   And I shall hear, though soft you tread above me,
   And all my dreams will warm and sweeter be.
   If you only tell me that you love me,
   Then I will sleep in peac until you come to me.

Just Before the Battle, Mother

Words and music by George F. Root

Slowly

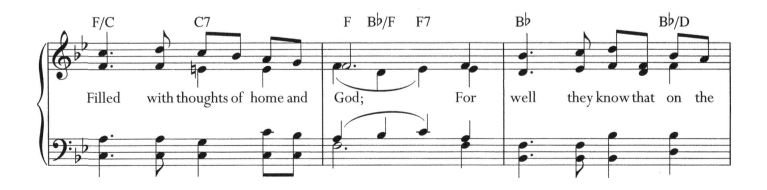

mor-row   Some   will sleep be-neath the   sod.

REFRAIN

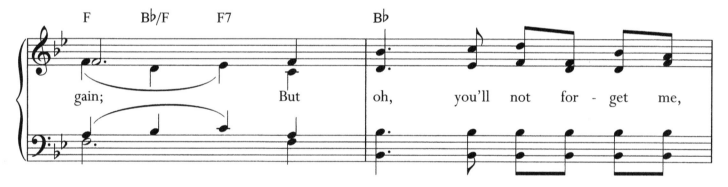

Fare - well, Moth- er, you may nev - er   Press   me to your heart a -

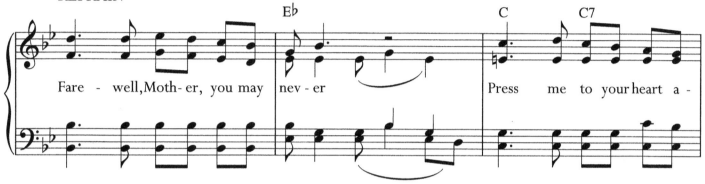

gain;   But   oh,   you'll   not   for - get   me,

Moth - er,   If   I'm num-bered with the   slain.

2. Hark, I hear the bugles sounding,
   'Tis the signal for the fight;
   Now may God protect us, Mother,
   As He ever does the right.
   Hear "The Battle Cry of Freedom,"
   How it swells upon the air;
   Oh, yes, we'll rally round the standard,
   Or we'll perish nobly there.
   Refrain

Memorial Day

Words and music by Susanna Blamire

2. Above the fields of former strife
   Now starts the waving grain,
   And all is bloom and light and life,
   Where heroes brave were slain.
   Bring sweetest flow'rs to deck the graves
   Where noble forms are laid;
   Bring amaranths and evergreens,
   Not those that early fade.

3. Plant myrtle and forget-me-nots,
   And roses white and red;
   Twine laurel wreaths about the stones
   Where sleep our martyred dead.
   And in the heart and on the lip
   Let those who lie away,
   Far off in swamps and in the sea,
   Be crowned with living bay.

The Minstrel Boy

Irish anthem

With spirit

1. The min-strel boy, to the war is gone, In the ranks of death you'll find him, His
2. The min-strel fell, but the foe-man's chain Could not bring his proud soul un - der. The

fa - ther's sword he has gird - ed on, And his wild harp slung be - hind him.
harp he loved ne'er spoke a - gain, For he tore its chords a - sun - der. And

"Land of song!" said the war - rior bard, "Tho' all the world be - tray thee, One
said "No chains shall sul - ly thee, thou soul of love and bra - ver-y! Thy

sword, at least thy rights shall guard, One faith - ful harp shall praise thee!"
songs were made for the pure and free, they shall nev - er sound in slav - 'ry!"

Rocked in the Cradle of the Deep

Words by Emma Willard
Music by Joseph P. Knight

Moderately slow

The Sailor's Grave

Words by Alfred, Lord Tennyson
English air

Moderately slow

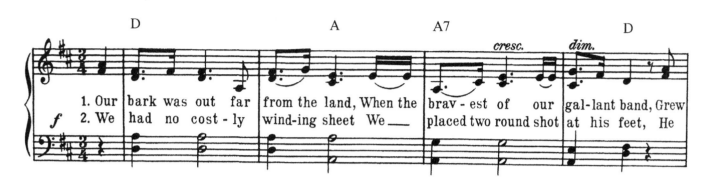

1. Our bark was out far from the land, When the brav-est of our gal-lant band, Grew
2. We had no cost-ly wind-ing sheet We ___ placed two round shot at his feet, He

death-ly pale and pined a-way, Like the twi-light of an au-tumn day; We
slept in ham-mock safe and sound, As a king in lawn shroud mar-ble bound; We

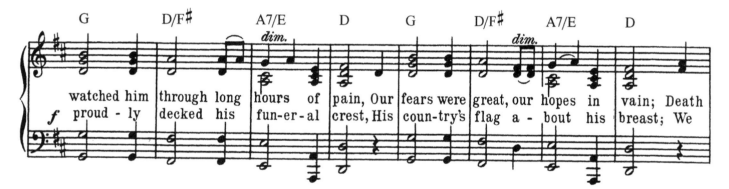

watched him through long hours of pain, Our fears were great, our hopes in vain; Death
proud-ly decked his fun-er-al crest, His coun-try's flag a-bout his breast; We

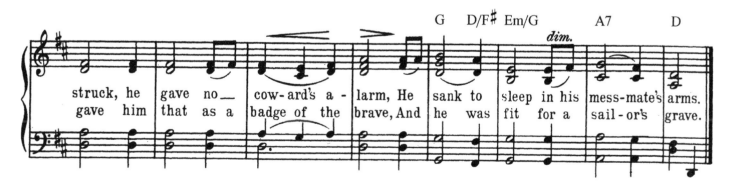

struck, he gave no ___ cow-ard's a-larm, He sank to sleep in his mess-mate's arms.
gave him that as a badge of the brave, And he was fit for a sail-or's grave.

Taps

United States Army Bugle Call

Slowly

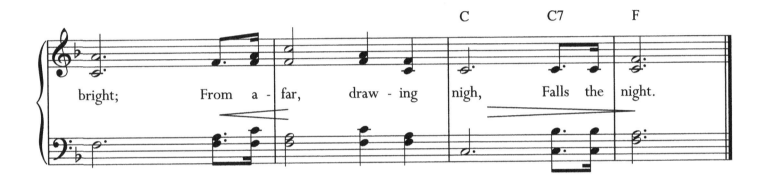

Fad - ing light dims the sight, And a star gems the sky, gleam ing

bright; From a - far, draw - ing nigh, Falls the night.

HYMNS AND PRAYERS

All Hail the Power of Jesus' Name

Words by Edward Perronet
Music by Oliver Holden

Majestically

1. All hail the power of Jesus' name! Let angels prostrate fall; Bring forth the royal diadem, And crown Him Lord of__ all! Bring forth the royal diadem, And crown Him Lord__ of all.

2. Let every kindred, every tribe,
On this terrestrial ball,
To Him all majesty ascribe,
And crown him Lord of all!
To Him all majesty ascribe,
And crown Him Lord of all.

All People That on Earth Do Dwell

(The Doxology)

Words by William Kethe
Words to "The Doxology" by Thomas Ken
Music by Louis Bourgeois

Moderately

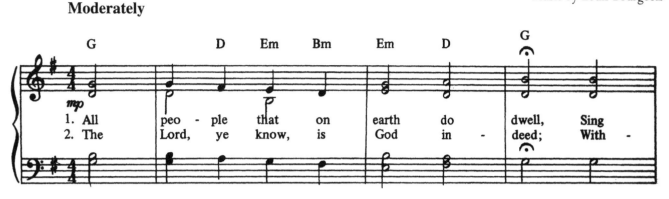

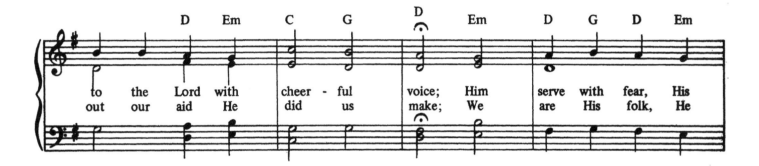

3. O enter then His gates with praise,
Approach with joy His courts unto:
Praise, laud and bless His name always,
For it is seemly so to do.

4. For why? the Lord our God is good;
His mercy is forever sure:
His truth at all times firmly stood,
And shall from age to age endure.

5. To Father, Son and Holy Ghost,
The God whom heaven and earth adore,
From men and from the angel-host
Be praise and glory evermore.

The Doxology
Praise God from whom all blessings flow,
Praise Him all creatures here below,
Praise Him above the heav'nly host,
Praise Father, Son, and Holy Ghost.

All Things Bright and Beautiful

Words by Cecil F. Alexander
Music by William H. Monk

Moderately fast

3. The cold wind in the winter,
   The pleasant summer sun,
   The ripe fruits in the garden,
   He made them ev'ry one:
   Refrain

4. The tall trees in the greenwood,
   The meadows where we play,
   The rushes by the water
   We gather ev'ry day:
   Refrain

5. He gave us eyes to see them,
   And lips that we might tell
   How great is God Almighty,
   Who has made all things well:
   Refrain

All Through the Night

Welsh lullaby

The Church's One Foundation

Words by Samuel J. Stone
Music by Samuel S. Wesley

Moderately

1. The church-'s one found - a - tion Is Je - sus Christ her
2. E - lect from ev - 'ry na - tion, Yet one from all the

Lord; She is His new cre - a - tion By
earth; Her char - ter new of sal - va - tion By One

wa - ter and the word; From heav'n He came and
Lord, one faith, one birth; From One ho - ly name she

sought her To be his ho - ly bride, With
bless - es, Par - takes one ho - ly food, And

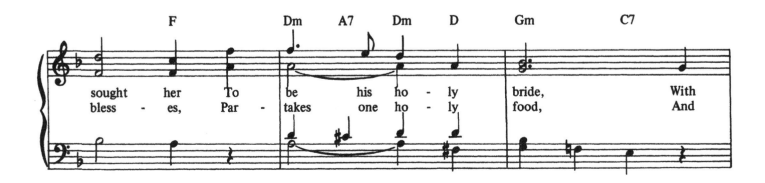

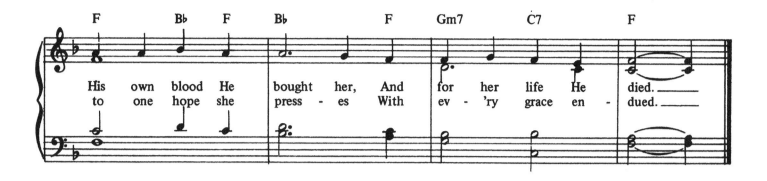

| F | B♭ | F | B♭ | F | Gm7 | C7 | F |

His own blood He | bought her, And | for her life He | died. _____
to one hope she | press - es With | ev - 'ry grace en - | dued. _____

3. Though with a scornful wonder
   Men see her sore oppressed,
   By schisms rent asunder,
   By heresies distressed,
   Yet saints their watch are keeping,
   Their cry goes up "How long?"
   And soon the night of weeping Shall
   be the morn of song.

4. 'Mid toil and tribulation,
   And tumult of her war,
   She waits the consummation
   Of peace for evermore;
   Till with the vision glorious
   Her longing eyes are blest,
   And the great Church victorious
   Shall be the Church at rest.

5. Yet she on earth hath union
   With God the Three in One
   And mystic sweet communion
   With those whose rest is won:
   O happy ones and holy!
   Lord give us grace that we
   Like them, the meek and lowly,
   On high may dwell with Thee.

Day Is Dying in the West

Words by Mary A. Lathbury
Music by William F. Sherwin

Quietly

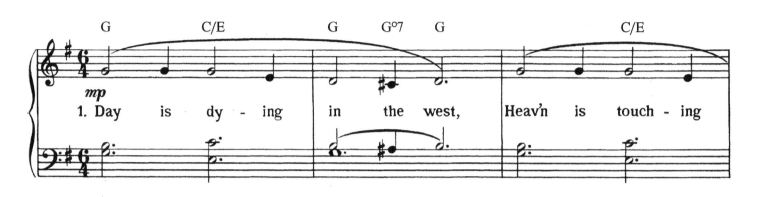

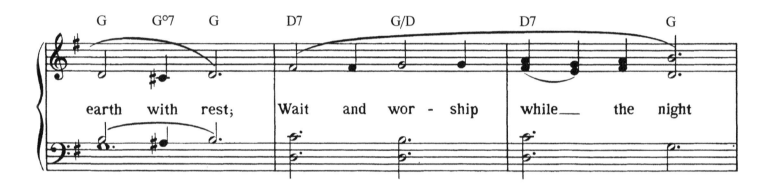

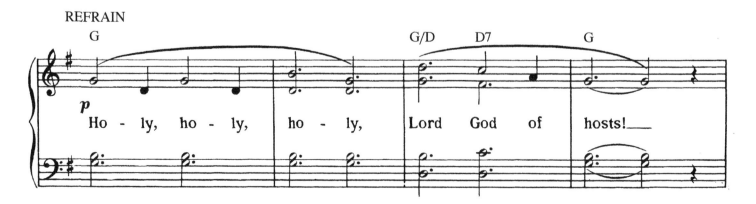

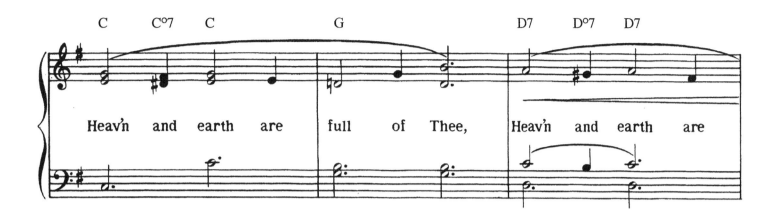

Heav'n and earth are full of Thee, Heav'n and earth are

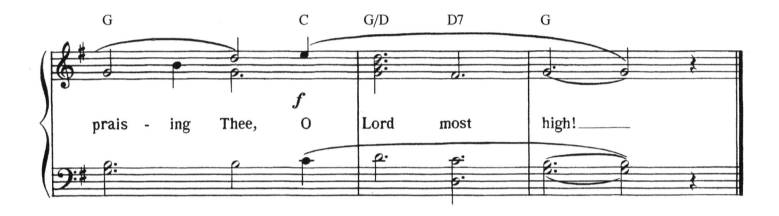

prais - ing Thee, O Lord most high!

2. Lord of life, beneath the dome
Of the universe, Thy home,
Gather us who seek Thy face
To the fold of Thy embrace,
For Thou art nigh.
Refrain

3. While the deepening shadows fall,
Heart of Love, enfolding all,
Through the glory and the grace
Of the stars that veil Thy face
Our hearts ascend.
Refrain

4. When, forever from our sight,
Pass the stars, the day, the night,
Lord of angels, on our eyes
Let eternal morning rise,
And shadows end.
Refrain

Faith of Our Fathers

Words by Frederick W. Faber
Music by Henri F. Hemy

Moderately slow

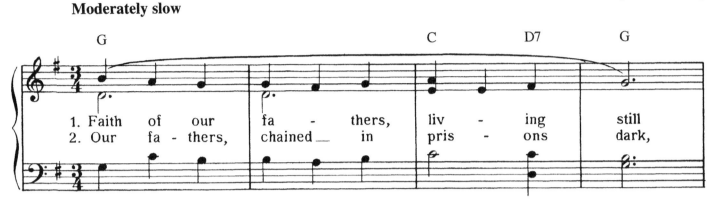

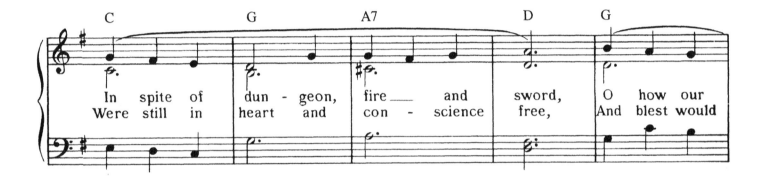

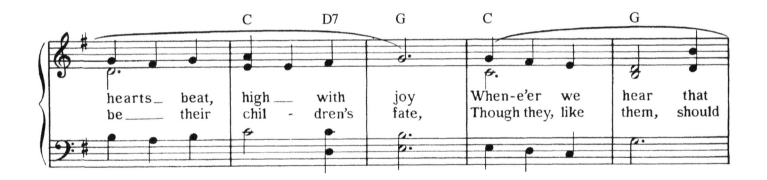

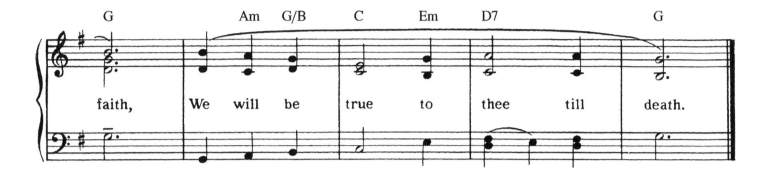

faith, We will be true to thee till death.

3. Faith of our fathers, faith and prayer
Shall keep our country brave and free,
And through the truth that comes from God,
Our land shall then indeed be free.
Faith of our fathers, holy faith,
We will be true to thee till death.

4. Faith of our fathers, we will love
Both friend and foe in all our strife,
And preach thee, too, as love knows how
By kindly words and virtuous life:
Faith of our fathers, holy faith,
We will be true to thee till death.

Glorious Things of Thee Are Spoken

Words by John Newton
Music by Franz Joseph Haydn

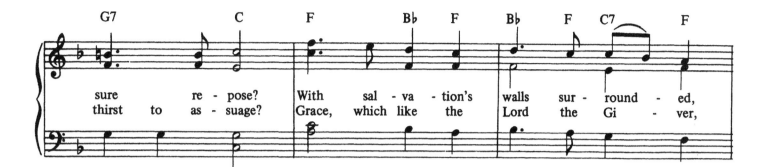

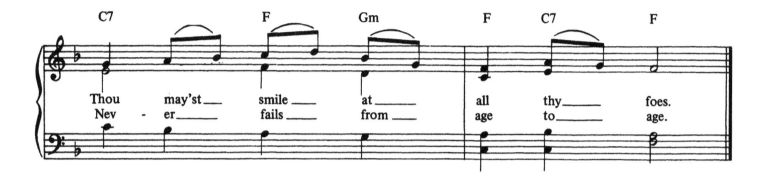

3. Round each habitation hov'ring,
   See the cloud and fire appear
   For a glory and a cov'ring,
   Showing that the Lord is near.
   Thus deriving from our banner
   Light by night and shade by day;
   Daily on the manna feeding
   Which He gives them when they pray.

4. Savior, if of Zion's city
   I, through grace, a member am,
   Let the world deride or pity,
   I will glory in Thy name:
   Fading is the worldling's pleasure.
   All his boasted pomp and show;
   Solid joys and lasting treasure
   None but Zion's children know.

God of Our Fathers

Words by Daniel C. Roberts
Music by George W. Warren

Majestically

1. God of our fathers, whose al-might-y hand
Leads forth in beau-ty all the star-ry band
Of shin-ing worlds in splen-dor through the skies,
Our grate-ful songs be-fore Thy throne a-rise.

2. Thy love divine hath led us in the past;
In this free land by Thee our lot is cast;
Be Thou our ruler, guardian, guide, and stay;
Thy word our law, Thy paths our chosen way.

3. From war's alarms, from deadly pestilence,
Be Thy strong arm our ever sure defense;
Thy true religion in our hearts increase,
Thy bounteous goodness nourish us in peace.

4. Refresh Thy people in their toilsome way,
Lead us from night to neverending day;
Fill all our lives with love and grace divine,
And glory, laud, and praise be ever Thine.

Holy, Holy, Holy

Words by Reginald Heber
Music by John B. Dykes

Moderately fast

1. Ho-ly, ho-ly, ho-ly! Lord God al-might-y! Earl-y in the morn-ing our song shall rise to Thee; Ho-ly, ho-ly ho-ly, mer-ci-ful and might-y! God in three per-sons, bless-ed trin-i-ty!

2. Ho-ly, ho-ly, ho-ly! all the saints a-dore Thee, Cast-ing down their gol-den crowns a-round the glass-y sea, Cher-u-bim and sera-phim, fall-ing down be-fore Thee, Who wert and art, and ev-er-more shalt be.

3. Holy, holy, holy!
   Though the darkness hide Thee,
   Though the eye of sinful man
   Thy glory may not see,
   Only Thou art holy;
   There is none beside Thee
   Perfect in power, in Love, and purity.

4. Holy, holy, holy!
   Lord God Almighty!
   All Thy works shall praise Thy name
   In earth and sky and sea:
   Holy, holy, holy!
   Merciful and mighty!
   God in three Persons, blessed trinity.

Lead, Kindly Light

Words by John H. Newman
Music by John B. Dykes

Freely

2. I was not ever thus, nor prayed that Thou
Should'st lead me on;
I loved to choose and see my path; but now
Lead Thou me on.
I loved the garish day, and, spite of fears,
Pride ruled my will: remember not past years.

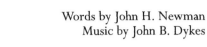

3. So long Thy power hath blest me, sure it still
Will lead me on,
O'er moor and fen, o'er crag and torrent, till
The night is gone;
And with the morn those angel faces smile,
Which I have loved long since, and lost awhile.

Lead Us Heavenly Father

Words by James Edmeston
Music by Friedrich Filitz

Moderately

1. Lead us, heaven-ly Fath - er, lead us O'er the world's tem - pes - tuous sea;
2. Sa - viour, breathe for - give - ness o'er us; All our weak - ness Thou dost know,

Guard us, guide us, keep us, feed us, For we have no help but Thee;
Thou didst tread this earth be - fore us, Thou didst feel its keen - est woe;

Yet pos - sess - ing ev - 'ry bless - ing If our God our Fath - er be.
Lone and drea - ry faint and wear - y, Through the de - sert Thou didst go.

3. Spirit of our God, descending,
Fill our hearts with heavenly joy,
Love with every passion blending,
Pleasure that can never cloy:
Thus provided, pardoned, guided,
Nothing can our peace destroy.

The Lord's My Shepherd

Words from *Scottish Psalter*
Music by Jessie Seymour Irvine

3. Yea, though I walk in death's dark vale,
   Yet will I fear no ill;
   For Thou art with me, and Thy rod
   And staff me comfort still.

4. My table Thou has furnished
   In presence of my foes;
   My head Thou dost with oil anoint,
   And my cup overflows.

5. Goodness and mercy all my life
   Shall surely follow me;
   And in God's house forevermore
   My dwelling-place shall be.

Nearer, My God, to Thee

Words by Sarah Flower Adams
Music by Lowell Mason

Sweetly

3. There let the way appear
   Steps unto heaven;
   All that Thou sendest me
   In mercy given;
   Angels to beckon me
   Nearer, my God, to Thee,
   Nearer, my God, to Thee,
   Nearer to Thee.

4. Then, with my waking thoughts
   Bright with Thy praise,
   Out of my stony griefs
   Bethel I'll raise;
   So by my woes to be
   Nearer, my God, to Thee,
   Nearer, my God, to Thee,
   Nearer to Thee.

5. Or if on joyful wing
   Cleaving the sky,
   Sun, moon, and stars forgot,
   Upward I fly,
   Still all my song shall be,
   Nearer, my God, to Thee,
   Nearer, my God, to Thee,
   Nearer to Thee.

A Mighty Fortress Is Our God

Words and music by Martin Luther

Majestically

3. And though this world, with devils filled,
   Should threaten to undo us,
   We will not fear, for God hath willed
   His truth to triumph through us:
   The Prince of Darkness grim,
   We tremble not for him;
   His rage we can endure,
   For lo, his doom is sure,
   One little word shall fell him.

4. That word above all earthly powers,
   No thanks to them, abideth;
   The Spirit and the gifts are ours
   Through Him Who with us sideth:
   Let goods and kindred go,
   This mortal life also;
   The body they may kill:
   God's truth abideth still,
   His kingdom is forever.

My Faith Looks Up to Thee

Words by Ray Palmer
Music by Lowell Mason

Moderately

1. My faith looks up to Thee, Thou Lamb of Cal-va-ry, Sav-ior di-vine! Now hear me
2. May Thy rich grace im-part Strength to my faint-ing heart, My zeal in-spire! As Thou hast

while I pray; Take all my guilt a-way; Oh, let me from this day Be whol-ly Thine.
died for me, Oh, may my love to Thee Pure, warm, and change-less be A liv-ing fire!

3. While life's dark maze I tread,
   And griefs around me spread,
   Be Thou my Guide;
   Bid darkness turn to day,
   Wipe sorrow's tears away,
   Nor let me ever stray
   From Thee aside.

4. When ends life's transient dream,
   When death's cold sullen stream
   Over me roll;
   Blest Savior, then in love,
   Fear and distrust remove;
   O bear me safe above,
   A ransomed soul!

Now the Day Is Over

Words by Sabine Baring-Gould
Music by Sir Joseph Barnby

Sweetly

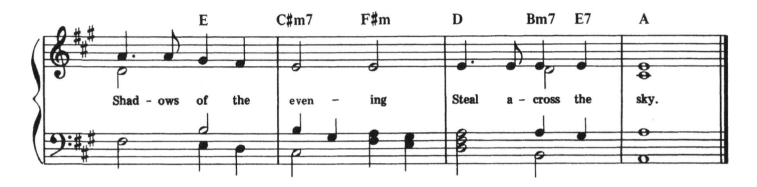

2. Jesus, give the weary
Calm and sweet repose;
With Thy tenderest blessing
May our eyelids close.

3. Grant to little children
Visions bright of Thee;
Guard the sailors tossing
On the deep blue sea.

4. Comfort every suff'rer
Watching late in pain;
Those who plan some evil,
From their sin restrain.

5. Through the long nightwatches
May Thine angels spread
Their white wings above me,
Watching round my bed.

6. When the morning wakens,
Then may I arise
Pure and fresh and sinless
In Thy holy eyes.

O God Our Help in Ages Past

Words by Isaac Watts
Music by William Croft

Moderately

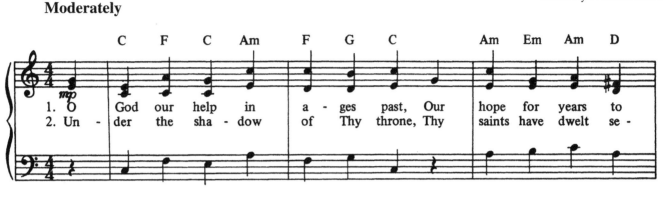

1. O God our help in a - ges past, Our hope for years to
2. Un - der the sha - dow of Thy throne, Thy saints have dwelt se -

come, our shel - ter from the stor - my blast, and our e - ter - nal home.
cure; Suf - fic - ient is Thine arm a - lone And our de - fence is sure.

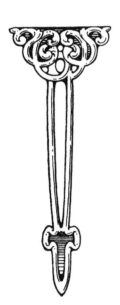

3. Before the hills in order stood,
   Or earth received her frame,
   From everlasting Thou art God,
   To endless years the same.

4. A thousand ages in Thy sight
   Are like an evening gone,
   Short as the watch that ends the night
   Before the rising sun.

5. Time, like an ever-rolling stream,
   Bears all its sons away,
   They fly forgotten, as a dream
   Dies at the opening day.

6. O God our help in ages past,
   Our hope for years to come,
   Be Thou our guard while troubles last,
   And our eternal home.

O Day of Rest and Gladness

Words by Christopher Wordsworth
German hymn

Moderately

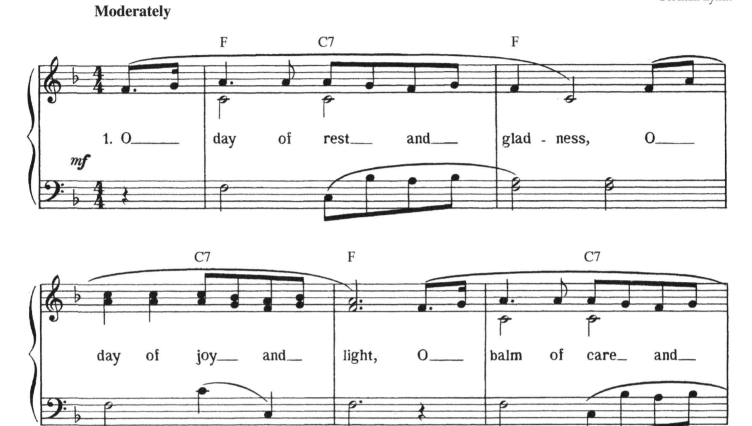

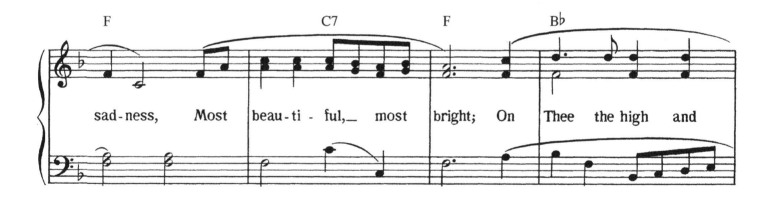

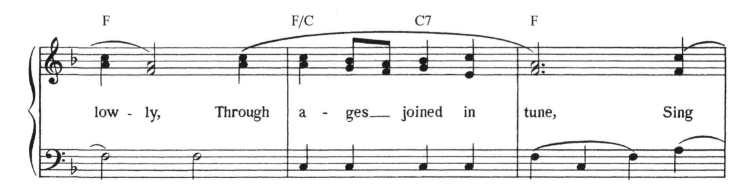

Ho - ly, Ho - ly, | Ho - ly, | To | the great God_ Tri - | une.

2. On thee at the creation
   The light first had its birth;
   On thee, for our salvation,
   Christ rose from depths of earth;
   On thee, our Lord, victorious,
   The Spirit sent from heav'n;
   And thus on thee, most glorious,
   A triple light was giv'n.

3. Today on weary nations
   The heavenly manna falls;
   To holy convocations
   The silver trumpet calls,
   Where gospel light is glowing
   With pure and radiant beams,
   And living water flowing
   With soul-refreshing streams.

4. New graces ever gaining
   From this our day of rest,
   We reach the rest remaining
   To spirits of the blest.
   To Holy Ghost be praises,
   To Father, and to Son;
   The Church her voice upraises
   To Thee, blest Three in One.

Onward, Christian Soldiers

Words by Sabine Baring-Gould
Music by Arthur Sullivan

Moderately

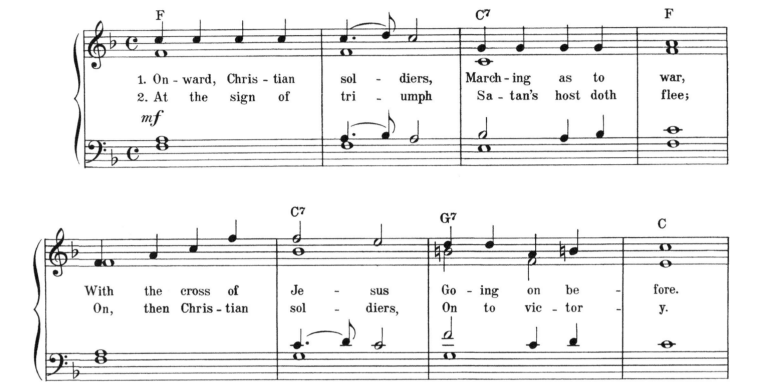

1. On - ward, Chris - tian sol - diers, March - ing as to war,
2. At the sign of tri - umph Sa - tan's host doth flee;

With the cross of Je - sus Go - ing on be - fore.
On, then Chris - tian sol - diers, On to vic - tor - y.

Christ, the roy - al Mas - ter, Leads a - gainst the foe;
Hell's foun - da - dion qui - var, At the shout of praise;

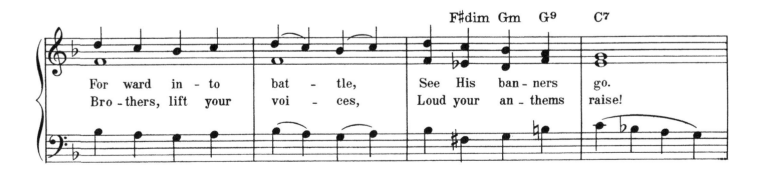

For - ward in - to bat - tle, See His ban - ners go.
Bro - thers, lift your voi - ces, Loud your an - thems raise!

2. Like a mighty army
   Moves the Church of God;
   Brothers, we are treading
   Where the saints have trod;
   We are not divided,
   All one body we,
   One in hope and doctrine,
   One in charity.
   Onward, Christian soldiers,
   Marching as to war,
   With the cross of Jesus
   Going on before.

3. Crowns and thrones may perish,
   Kingdoms rise and wane,
   But the Church of Jesus
   Constant will remain;
   Gates of hell can never
   'Gainst that Church prevail;
   We have Christ's own promise,
   And that cannot fail.
   Onward, Christian soldiers,
   Marching as to war,
   With the cross of Jesus
   Going on before.

4. Onward, then, ye people,
   Join our happy throng,
   Blend with ours your voices
   In the triumph song;
   Glory, laud, and honor
   Unto Christ the King,
   This through countless ages
   Men and angels sing.
   Onward, Christian soldiers,
   Marching as to war,
   With the cross of Jesus
   Going on before.

When I Survey the Wondrous Cross

Words by Isaac Watts
Music by Edward Miller

Moderately

1. When I _____ sur - vey the won - drous cross, On which the
2. For - bid ____ it Lord, that I should boast, Save in the

Prince of Glo - ry died, ____ My rich - est gain I
death of Christ ____ my God; ____ All the vain things that

count ____ but loss and pour con - tempt on all _____ my pride.
charm ____ me most, I sac - ri - fice them to _____ His blood.

3. See from His head, His hands, His feet
   Sorrow and love flow mingled down;
   Did e'er such love and sorrow meet,
   Or thorns compose so rich a crown?

4. His dying crimson, like a robe,
   Spreads o'er His body on the tree;
   Then am I dead to all the globe,
   And all the globe is dead to me.

5. Were the whole realm of nature mine,
   That were a present far too small;
   Love so amazing, so divine,
   Demands my soul, my life, my all.

BELOVED SPIRITUALS

Blow Your Trumpet, Gabriel

American spiritual

With movement

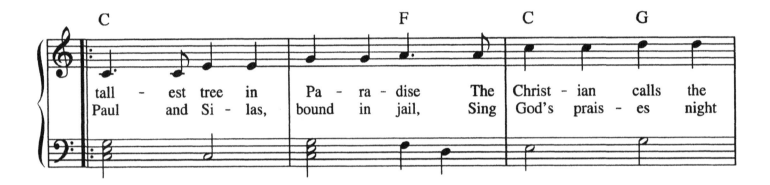

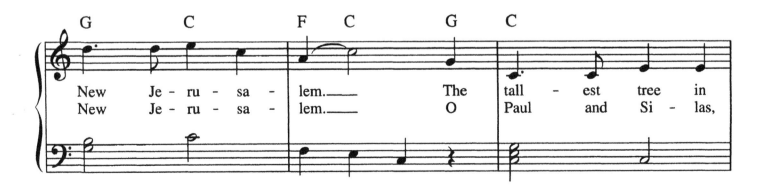

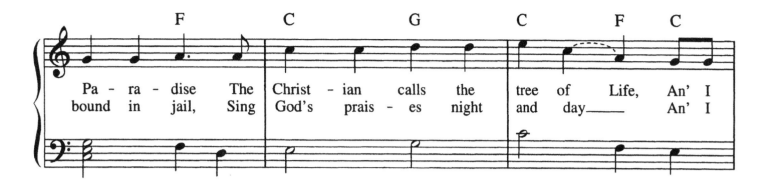

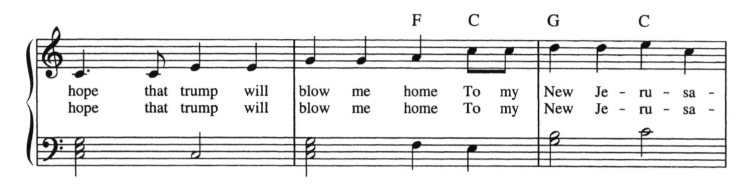

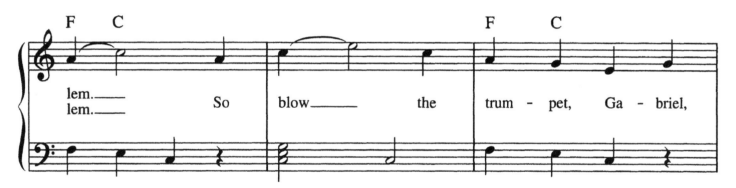

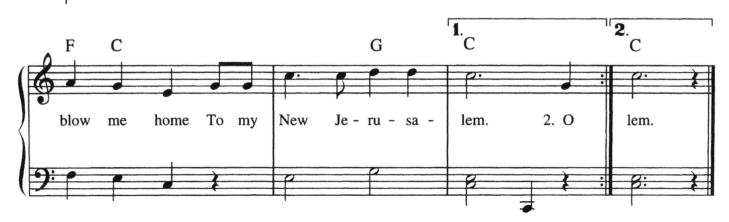

Deep River

American spiritual

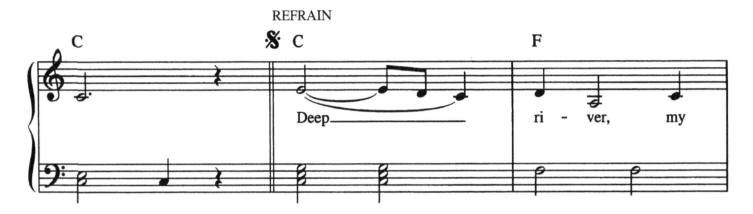

1. Oh, don't you want to go to that gos - pel

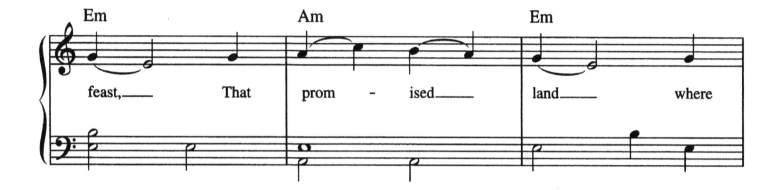

feast, That prom - ised land where

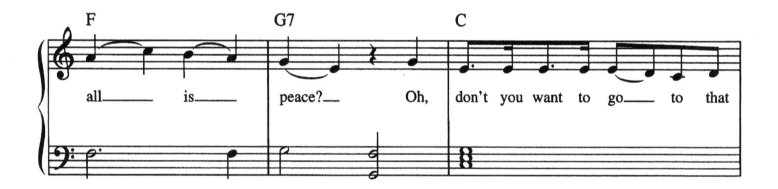

all is peace? Oh, don't you want to go to that

prom - ised land That land where all is peace?

D.S. al Fine

2. I'll go up to Heaven and take my seat,
And cast my crown at Jesus' feet.
When I go up to Heaven I'll walk about,
That land where all is peace.
Refrain

Git on Board, Little Children

American spiritual

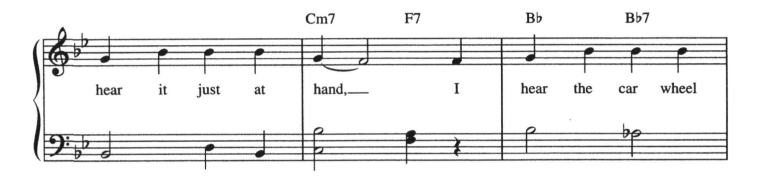

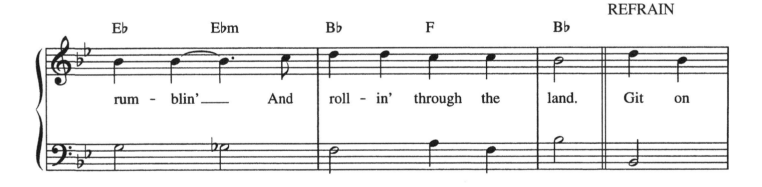

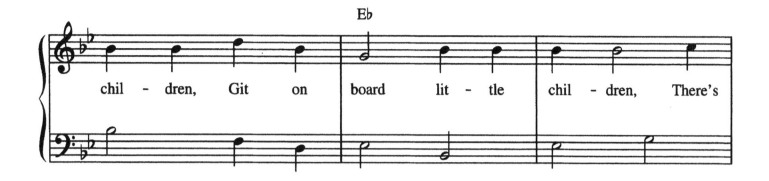

chil - dren, Git on board lit - tle chil - dren, There's

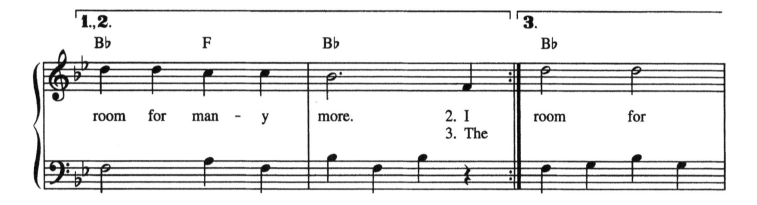

1.,2. room for man - y more. 2. I / 3. The   **3.** room for

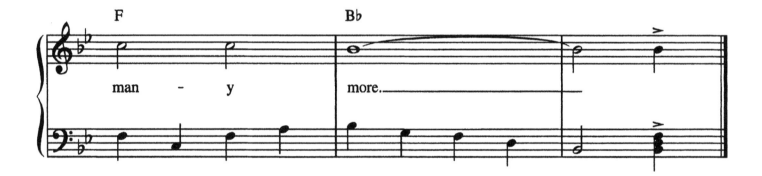

man - y more.

2. I hear that train a-comin',
   She's comin' round the curve,
   She's loosened all her steam and brakes
   And straining every nerve.
   Refrain

3. The fare is cheap and all can go,
   The rich and poor are there,
   No second class aboard this train,
   No difference in the fare.
   Refrain

Give Me That Old Time Religion

American spiritual

Energetically

Give me that old time re-lig-ion, Give me that old time re-

lig-ion, Give me that old time re-lig-ion, It's good e-nough for me.

Fine

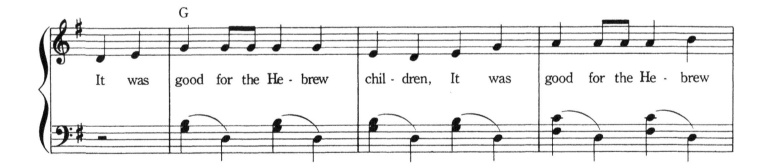

It was good for the He-brew chil-dren, It was good for the He-brew

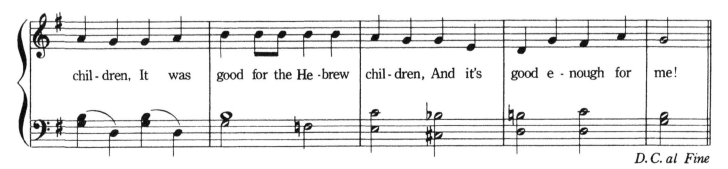

chil-dren, It was good for the He-brew chil-dren, And it's good e-nough for me!

D.C. al Fine

He's Got the Whole World in His Hands

American spiritual

With a steady beat

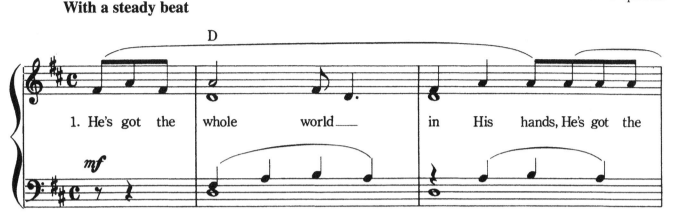

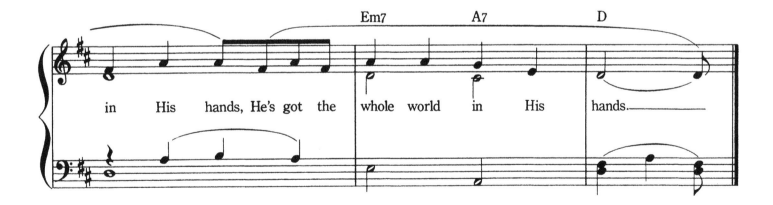

2. He's got the earth and sky in His hands, *etc.*
   He's got the whole world in His hands.

3. He's got the land and sea in His hands, *etc.*
   He's got the whole world in His hands.

4. He's got the little bitty baby in His hands, *etc.*
   He's got the whole world in His hands.

5. He's got you and me, brother, in His hands, *etc.*
   He's got the whole world in His hands.

6. He's got the gamblin' man in His hands, *etc.*
   He's got the whole world in His hands.

7. He's got the whole world in His hands, *etc.*
   He's got the whole world in His hands.

Kumbayah
(Come by Here)

Nigerian-American spiritual

Slowly

1. Kum ba yah, my Lord,_____ Kum ba yah!_____

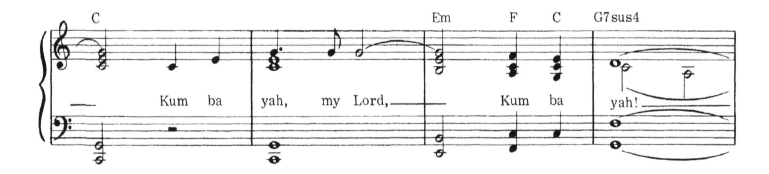

Kum ba yah, my Lord,_____ Kum ba yah!

Kum ba yah, my Lord,_____ Kum ba yah!_____

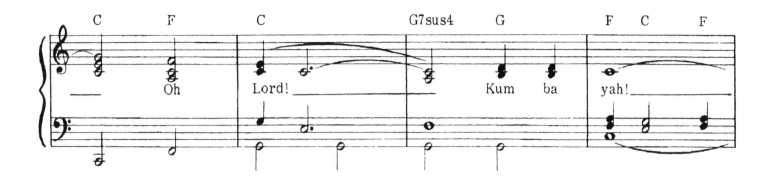

Oh Lord! Kum ba yah!

2. Someone's crying, Lord, kumbayah, *etc.*

3. Someone's singing, Lord, kumbayah, *etc.*

4. Someone's praying, Lord, kumbayah, *etc.*

5. Someone's sleeping, Lord, kumbayah, *etc.*

Joshua Fit the Battle of Jericho

American spiritual

With spirit

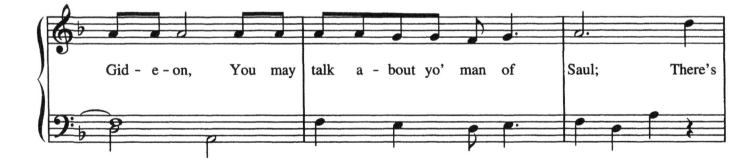

none like good old Josh - u - a At the bat - tle of Je - ri -

cho. 2. Up___ to the walls of Je - ri - cho He

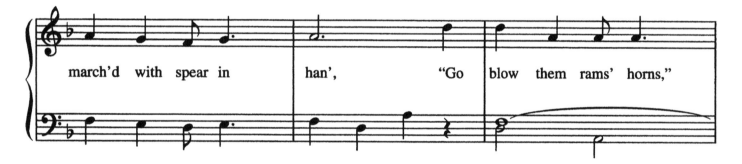

march'd with spear in han', "Go blow them rams' horns,"

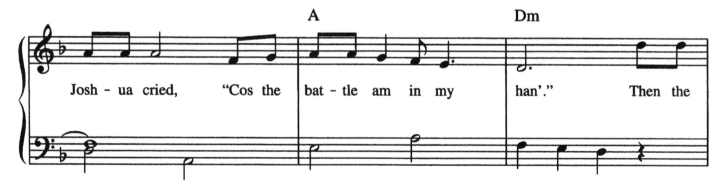

Josh - ua cried, "Cos the bat - tle am in my han'." Then the

lam' ram sheep horns 'gin to blow,— Trum - pets be - gin to

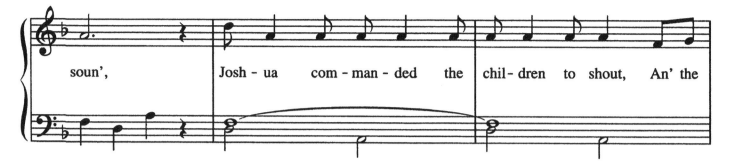

soun', Josh-ua com-man-ded the chil-dren to shout, An' the

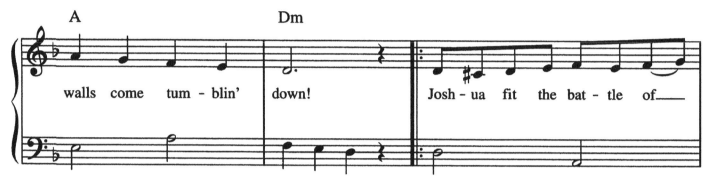

A — Dm

walls come tum-blin' down! Josh-ua fit the bat-tle of—

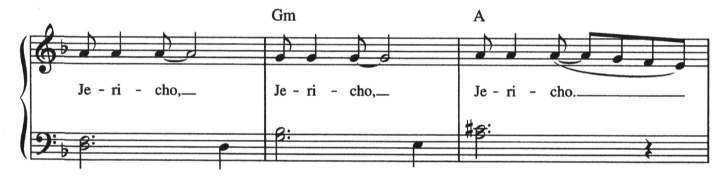

Gm — A

Je-ri-cho,— Je-ri-cho,— Je-ri-cho.—

Dm — 1. A

Josh-ua fit the bat-tle of— Je-ri-cho,— An' the walls come tum-blin'

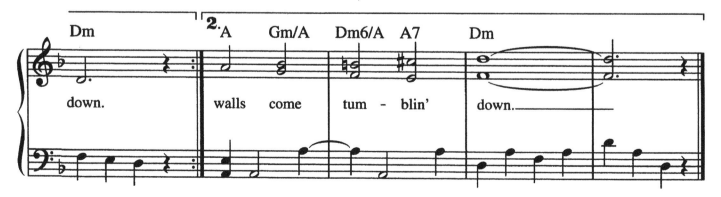

Dm — 2. A Gm/A Dm6/A A7 Dm

down. walls come tum-blin' down.—

Let Us Break Bread Together

(Communion Hymn)

American spiritual

Moderately

Let us break bread to - geth - er on our knees

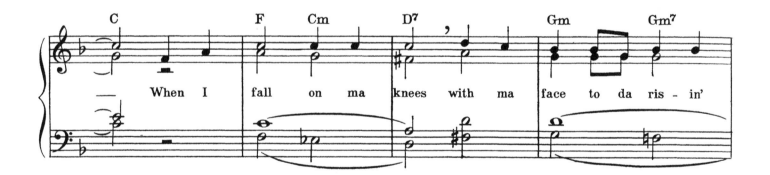

Let us break bread to - geth - er on our knees

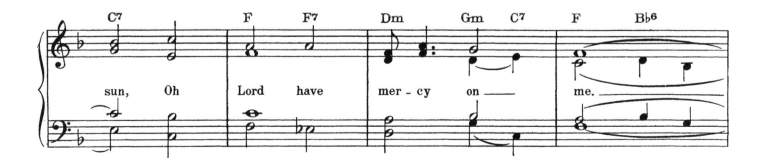

When I fall on ma knees with ma face to da ris - in'

sun, Oh Lord have mer - cy on me.

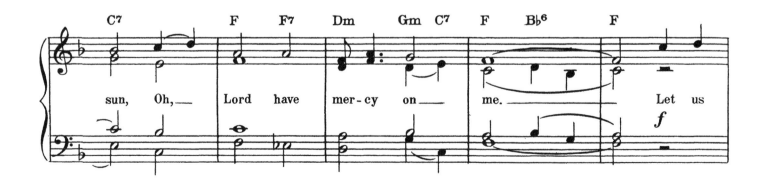

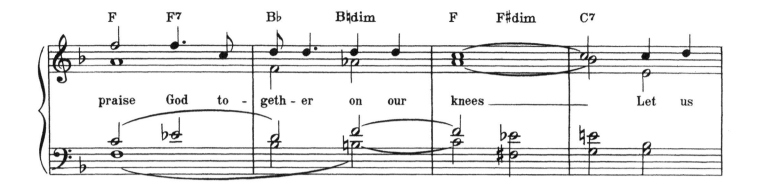

praise God to - geth - er on our knees _____ Let us

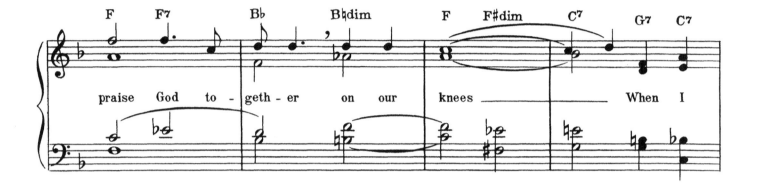

praise God to - geth - er on our knees _____ When I

fall on ma knees with ma face to da ris - in' sun, Oh ___

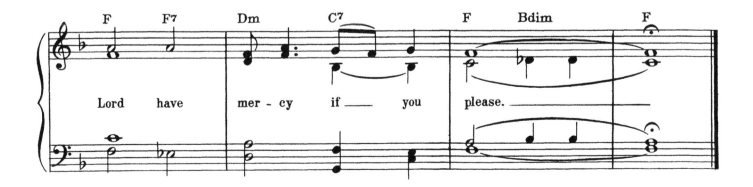

Lord have mer - cy if ___ you please. _____

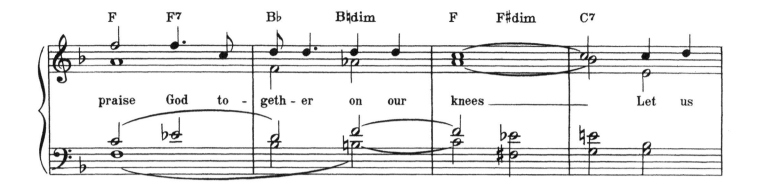

Let My People Go

American spiritual

Slowly

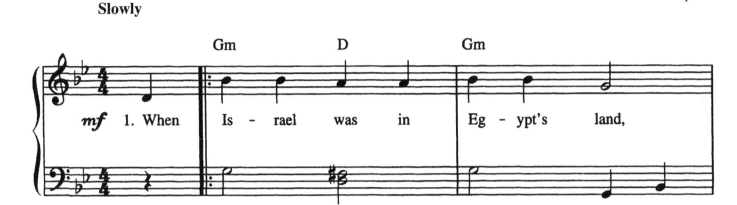

mf 1. When Is - rael was in Eg - ypt's land,

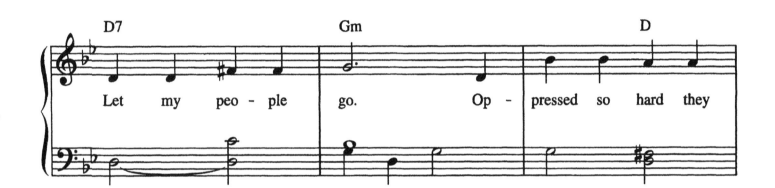

Let my peo - ple go. Op - pressed so hard they

could not stand Let my peo - ple go.

REFRAIN

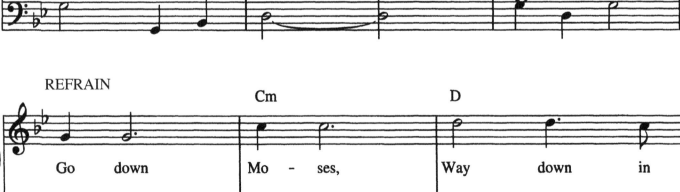

Go down Mo - ses, Way down in

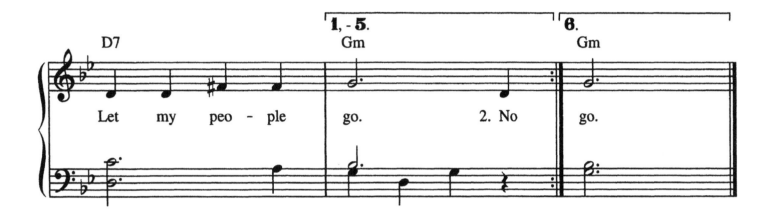

2. No more shall they in bondage toil,
Let my people go.
Let them come out with Egypt's spoil.
Let my people go.
Refrain

3. As Israel stood by the waterside,
At God's command it did divide,
Refrain

4. And when they reached the other shore,
They sang a song of triumph o'er.
Refrain

5. Then Pharaoh said he'd go across,
But Pharaoh and his host were lost.
Refrain

6. Your foes shall not before you stand,
And you'll posess fair Canaan's land.
Refrain

Nobody Knows the Trouble I've Seen

American spiritual

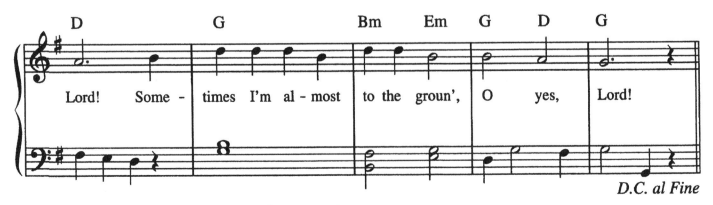

One More River to Cross

American spiritual

Moderately

Oh, was-n't that a wide riv-er, Riv-er of Jor-dan, Lord, Wide riv-er, There's one more riv-er to

1. F N.C. cross, Oh, was-n't that a **2. & Fine** F cross. 1. Oh, you got Je - sus, hold Him fast, One more riv-er to strong-er than an i - ron band, One more riv-er to

cross, Oh, bet - ter love was nev-er told, One more riv-er to cross, 'Tis sweet-er than that hon-ey comb, One more riv-er to **1.** F cross. 2. 'Tis **2.** F N.C. *D.S. al Fine* cross. Oh, was-n't that a

Sometimes I Feel Like a Motherless Child

American spiritual

Slowly

1. Some-times I feel like a moth-er-less child, Some-times I feel like a moth-er-less child,
2. Some-times I feel like I has no friend, Some-times I feel like I has no friend,

Some-times I feel like a moth-er-less child, A long ways from home,
Some-times I feel like I has no friend, A long ways from home,

long ways from home, O Law - dy, a long ways from home.
long ways from home, O Law - dy, a long ways from home.

3. Sometimes I wish that I'd never been born,
Sometimes I wish that I'd never been born,
Sometimes I wish that I'd never been born,
I know my time ain't long,
I know my time ain't long,
O Lawdy, I know my time ain't long.

4. Sometimes I feel like a feather in the air,
Sometimes I feel like a feather in the air,
Sometimes I feel like a feather in the air,
A long ways from home,
A long ways from home,
O Lawdy, a long ways from home.

5. Sometimes I feel like I'm almost gone,
Sometimes I feel like I'm almost gone,
Sometimes I feel like I'm almost gone,
A long ways from home,
A long ways from home,
O Lawdy, a long ways from home.

Steal Away

American spiritual

Slowly

Steal a-way, Steal a-way, Steal a-way to Je-sus:

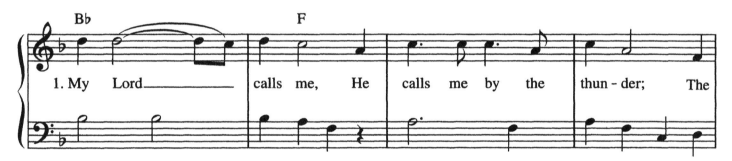

Steal a-way, Steal a-way home, I ain't got long to stay here. *Fine*

1. My Lord___ calls me, He calls me by the thun-der; The

trum-pet sounds___ with-in___ my soul I ain't got long to stay here.

D.C. al Fine

2. Green trees are bending,
Poor sinners stand trembling,
The trumpet sounds within my soul
I ain't got long to stay here.
Refrain

3. My Lord calls me,
He calls me by the lightning.
The trumpet sounds within my soul
I ain't got long to stay here.
Refrain

Standin' in the Need of Prayer

American spiritual

Moderato

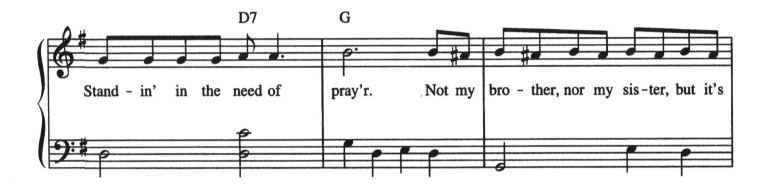

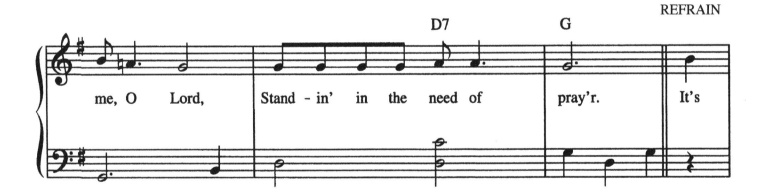

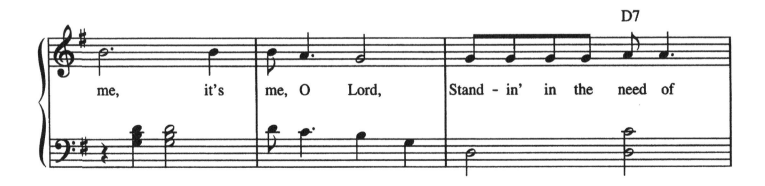

2. Not the preacher, nor the deacon, but it's me, O Lord,
   Standin' in the need of pray'r.
   Refrain

3. Not my father, nor my mother, but it's me, O Lord,
   Standin' in the need of pray'r.
   Refrain

4. Not the stranger, nor my neighbor, but it's me, O Lord,
   Standin' in the need of pray'r.
   Refrain

Swing Low, Sweet Chariot

American spiritual

With movement

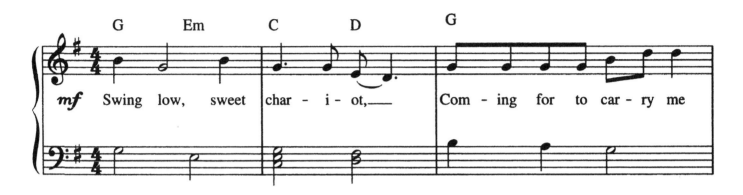

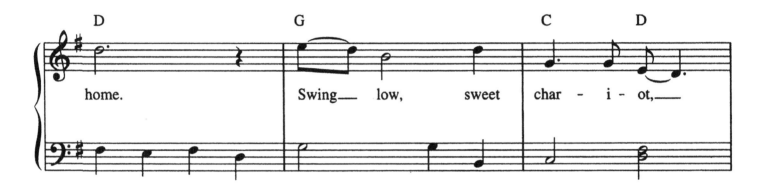

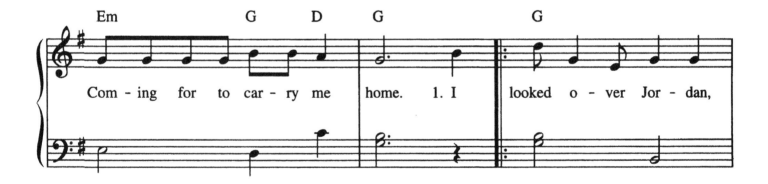

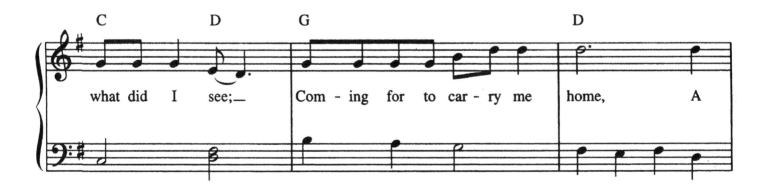

band__ of an - gels   com - ing af - ter me,__   Com - ing for to car - ry me

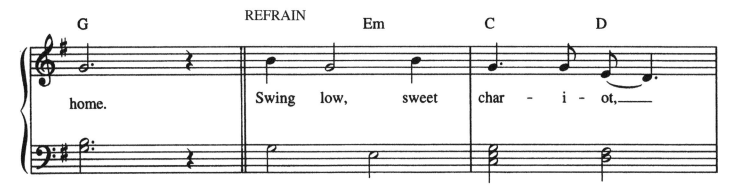

REFRAIN

home.   Swing low,   sweet   char - i - ot,__

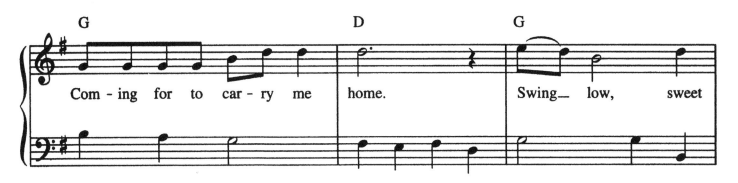

Com - ing for to car - ry me   home.   Swing__ low,   sweet

char - i - ot,__   Com - ing for to car - ry me   home. 2. If   home.

2. If you get there before I do,
   Coming for to carry me home,
   Tell all my friends I'm coming after you,
   Coming for to carry me home.
   Refrain

3. I'm sometimes up and sometimes down,
   Coming for to carry me home,
   But still my soul feels heaven-bound,
   Coming for to carry me home.
   Refrain

When the Saints Go Marching In

American spiritual

With a steady beat

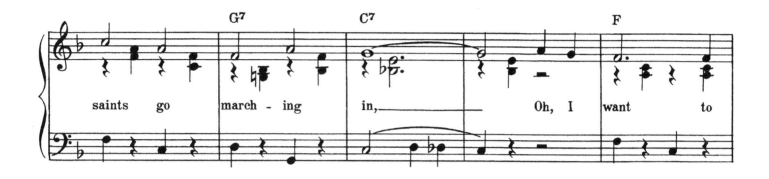

saints go | march - ing | in,_____ | Oh, I | want to

be | in that | num - ber,_____ | When the | saints go

march - ing | in._____ | 2. So I | I want to

3. Come and join me in my journey,
   'Cause it's time that we begin;
   And we'll be there for that judgment,
   When the saints go marching in.
   Chorus

Additional Choruses

I want to join the heav'nly band,
I want to join the heav'nly band,
Want to hear the trumpets a-blowing,
When the saints go marching in.

I want to see those pearly gates,
I want to see those pearly gates,
Want to see those gates standing open,
When the saints go marching in.

GOSPEL PRAISE

Abide with Me

Words by Henry F. Lyte
Music by William H. Monk

Slowly

1. A - bide with me; fast falls the e - ven - tide;
The dark - ness deep - ens, Lord, with me a - bide!
When oth - er help - ers fail, and com - forts flee,
Help of the help - less, O a - bide with me.

2. Swift to its close ebbs out life's little day;
Earth's joys grow dim, its glories pass away,
Change and decay in all around I see;
O Thou who changest not, abide with me.

3. I need Thy presence every passing hour;
What but Thy grace can foil the tempter's power?
Who like Thyself my guide and stay can be?
Through cloud and sunshine, O abide with me.

4. I fear no foe, with Thee at hand to bless;
Ills have no weight, and tears no bitterness:
Where is death's sting? where, grave, thy victory?
I triumph still if Thou abide with me.

5. Hold thou Thy cross before my closing eyes,
Shine through the gloom, and point me to the skies:
Heav'n's morning breaks, and earth's vain shadows flee;
In life and death, O Lord, abide with me.

Blessed Assurance

Words by Fanny Crosby
Music by Mrs. Joseph F. Knapp

1. Bless-ed as-sur-ance, Je-sus is mine! O what a fore-taste of glo-ry di-vine! Heir of sal-va-tion, pur-chase of God, Born of His Spir-it, washed in His blood.

REFRAIN
This is my sto-ry, this is my song, Prais-ing my Sav-ior all the day long; This is my sto-ry, this is my song, Prais-ing my Sav-ior all the day long.

2. Perfect submission, perfect delight,
Visions of rapture now burst on my sight;
Angels descending, bring from above,
Echoes of mercy, whispers of love.
Refrain

3. Perfect submission, all is at rest,
I in my Savior am happy and blessed,
Watching and waiting, looking above,
Filled with His goodness, lost in His love.
Refrain

He Leadeth Me

Words by Joseph H. Gilmore
Music by William B. Bradbury

Moderately

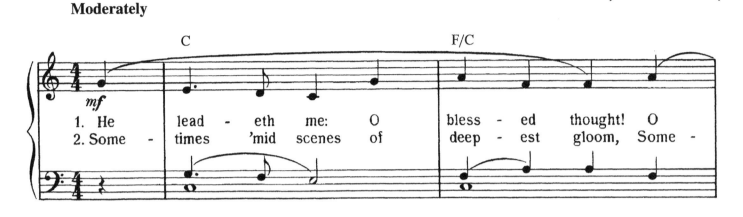

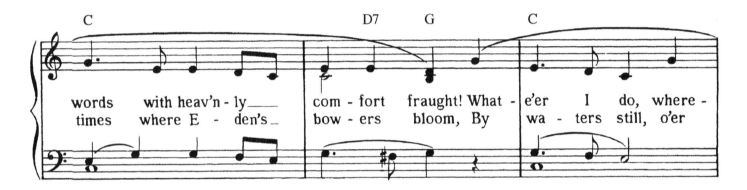

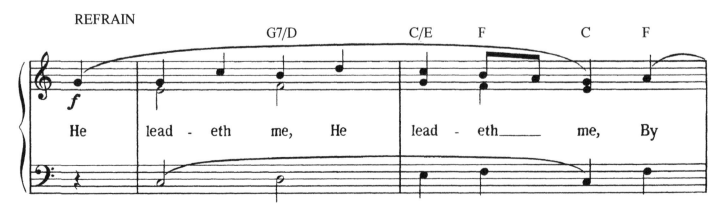

His own hand_ He_ lead - eth me; His faith - ful fol - lower

I would_ be, For by His hand_ He_ lead - eth me.

3. Lord, I would place my hand in Thine,
   Nor ever murmur nor repine;
   Content, whatever lot I see,
   Since 'tis my God that leadeth me.
   Refrain

4. And when my task on earth is done,
   When, by Thy grace, the victory's won,
   E'en death's cold wave I will not flee,
   Since God through Jordan leadeth me.
   Refrain

How Sweet the Name of Jesus Sounds

Words by John Newton
Music by Alexander R. Reinagle

Moderately fast

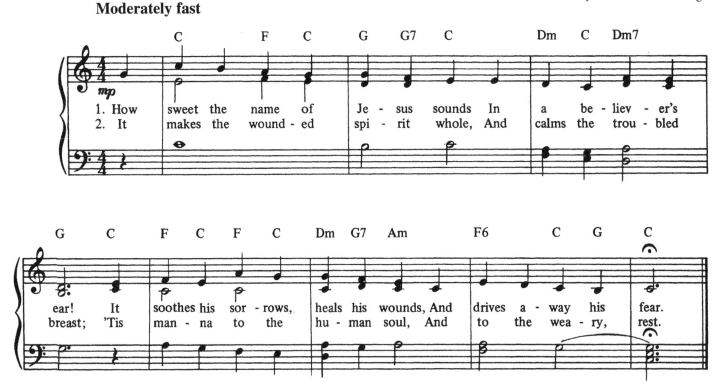

1. How sweet the name of Je - sus sounds In a be - liev - er's
2. It makes the wound - ed spi - rit whole, And calms the trou - bled

ear! It soothes his sor - rows, heals his wounds, And drives a - way his fear.
breast; 'Tis man - na to the hu - man soul, And to the wea - ry, rest.

3. Dear name! the rock on which I build,
   My shield and hiding place,
   My never-failing treasury filled
   With boundless stores of grace.

4. Jesus! my Shepherd, Brother, Friend,
   My Prophet, Priest and King,
   My Lord, my Life, my Way, my End,
   Accept the praise I bring.

5. Weak is the effort of my heart,
   And cold my warmest thought;
   But when I see Thee as Thou art,
   I'll praise Thee as I ought.

6. Till then I would Thy love proclaim
   With ev'ry fleeting breath;
   And may the music of Thy name
   Refresh my soul in death.

I Need Thee Every Hour

Words by Annie Sherwood Hawks
Music by Robert Lowry

Moderately

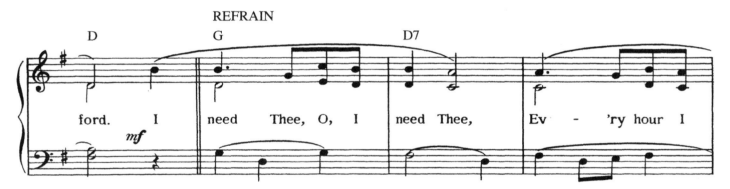

2. I need Thee every hour;
   Stay Thou near by;
   Temptations lose their power
   When Thou art nigh.
   Refrain

3. I need Thee every hour.
   In joy or pain,
   Come quickly and abide.
   Or life is vain.
   Refrain

4. I need Thee every hour;
   Teach me Thy will,
   And Thy rich promises
   In me fulfill.
   Refrain

I Love to Tell the Story

Words by Katherine Hankey
Music by William G. Fischer

Moderately

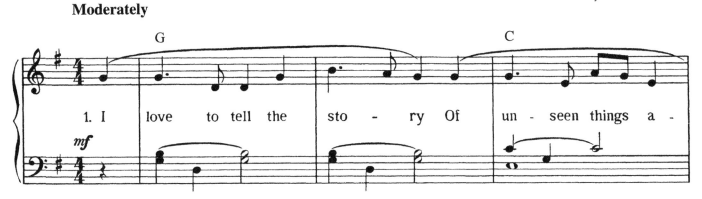

1. I love to tell the sto - ry Of un - seen things a -

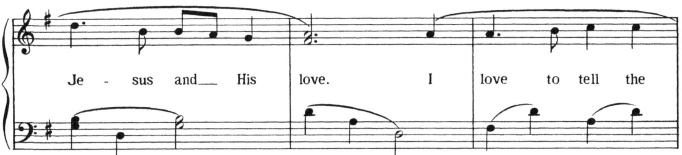

bove, Of Je - sus and His glo - ry, Of___

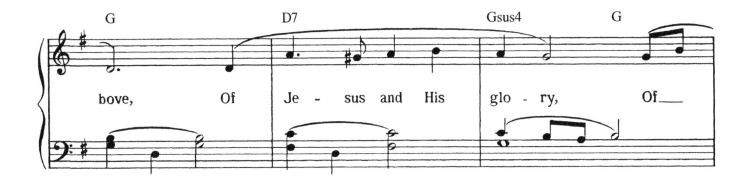

Je - sus and___ His love. I love to tell the

sto - ry, Be - cause I know 'tis___ true, It

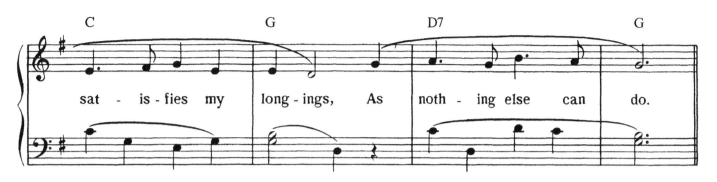

sat - is - fies my long-ings, As noth - ing else can do.

REFRAIN

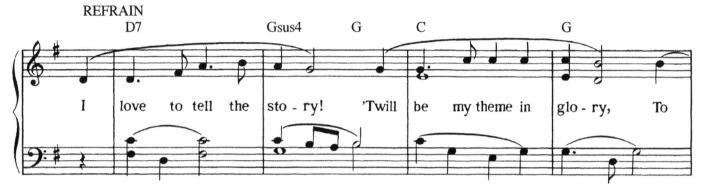

I love to tell the sto - ry! 'Twill be my theme in glo - ry, To

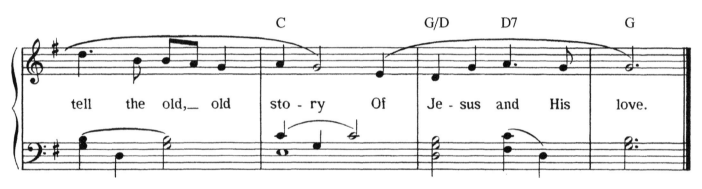

tell the old,__ old sto - ry Of Je - sus and His love.

2. I love to tell the story;
   More wonderful it seems
   Than all the golden fancies
   Of all our golden dreams.
   I love to tell the story,
   It did so much for me;
   And that is just the reason
   I tell it now to thee.
   Refrain

3. I love to tell the story;
   'Tis pleasant to repeat
   What seems, each time I tell it,
   More wonderfully sweet.
   I love to tell the story;
   For some have never heard
   The message of salvation
   From God's own holy word.
   Refrain

4. I love to tell the story;
   For those who know it best
   Seem hungering and thirsting
   To hear it like the rest.
   And when, in scenes of glory,
   I sing the new, new song,
   'Twill be the old, old story,
   That I have loved so long.
   Refrain

In the Sweet By and By

Words by S. Fillmore Bennet
Music by J.P. Webster

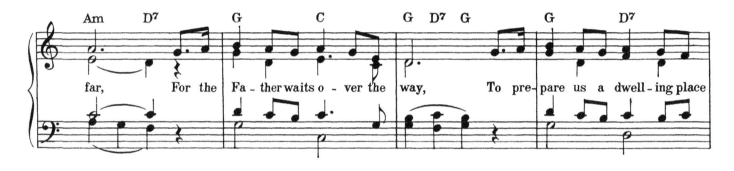

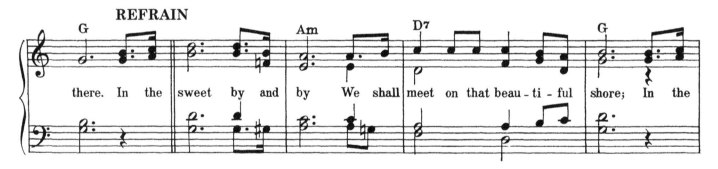

2. We shall sing on that beautiful shore
The melodious songs of the blessed,
And our spirits shall sorrow no more,
Not a sigh for the blessing of rest.
Refrain

3. To our bountiful Father above,
We will offer the tribute of praise,
For the glorious gift of His love,
And the blessings that hallow our days.
Refrain

Jerusalem, the Golden

Words by Bernard of Morlaix
Music by Alexander Ewing

Moderately

1. Je - ru - sa - lem the gold - en, With milk and hon - ey blessed, Be -
2. They stand, those halls of Zi - on, Con - ju - bi - lant with song, And

neath thy con - tem - pla - tion Sink heart and voice op - pressed. I
bright with many an an - gel And all the mar - tyr throng; The

know not O I know not What joys a - wait us there, What
Prince is ev - er in them, The day - light is se - rene, The

ra - dian - cy of glo - ry, What light be - yond com - pare.
pas - tures of the bless - ed Are decked in glo - rious sheen.

3. There is the throne of David,
And there, from care released,
The shout of them that triumph,
The song of them that feast:
And they who, with their Leader,
Have conquered in the fight,
Forever and forever
Are clad in robes of white.

4. Jerusalem the glorious,
The home of God's elect;
O dear and future vision
That eager hearts expect!
Jesus, in mercy bring us
To that dear land of rest,
Who art, with God the Father
And Spirit, ever blessed.

Jesus, Lover of My Soul

Words by Charles Wesley
Music by Simeon B. Marsh

Sweetly

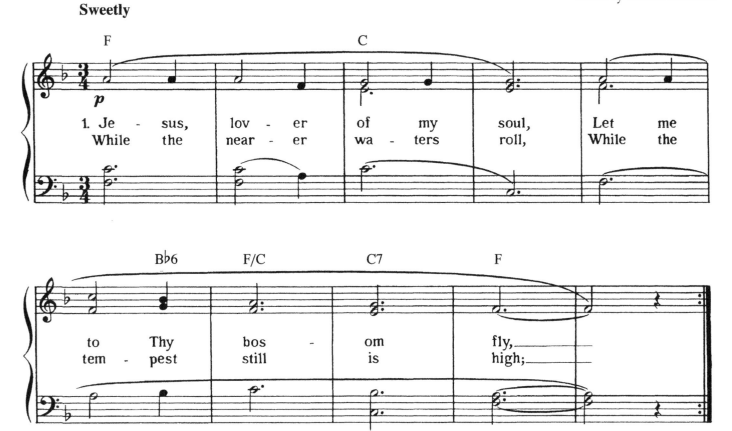

1. Je - sus, lov - er of my soul, Let me
While the near - er wa - ters roll, While the

to Thy bos - om fly,
tem - pest still is high;

Hide me, O my Sav - ior, hide

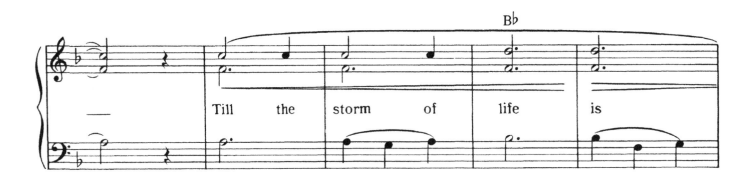

Till the storm of life is

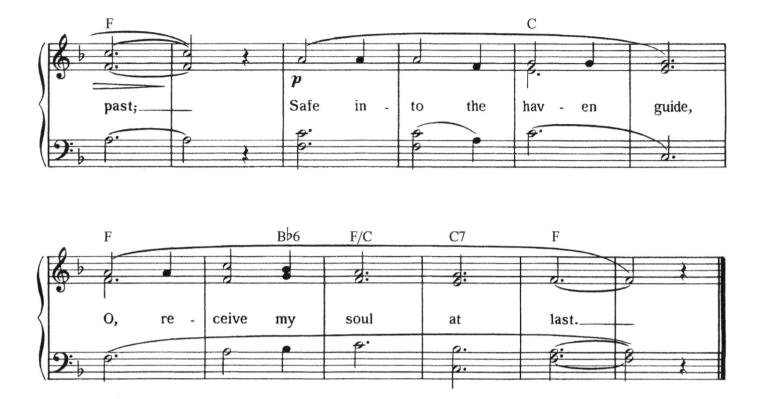

past;_____ Safe in - to the hav - en guide,

O, re - ceive my soul at last._____

2. Other refuge have I none,
Hangs my helpless soul on Thee;
Leave, ah, leave me not alone,
Still support and comfort me!
All my trust on Thee is stayed,
All my help from Thee I bring;
Cover my defenseless head
With the shadow of Thy wing.

3. Plenteous grace with Thee is found,
Grace to cleanse from all my sin;
Let the healing streams abound,
Make and keep me pure within.
Thou of life the fountain art;
Freely let me take of Thee;
Spring Thou up within my heart,
Rise to all eternity.

Jesus Loves Me, This I Know

Words by Anna B. Warner
Music by William B. Bradbury

Sweetly

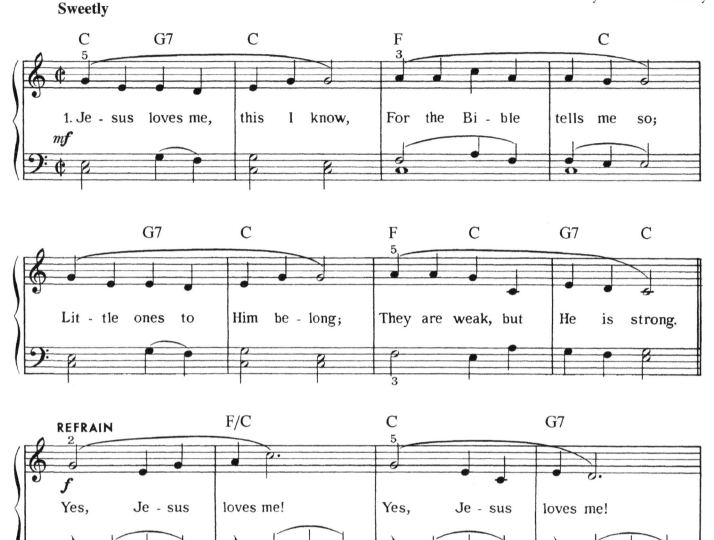

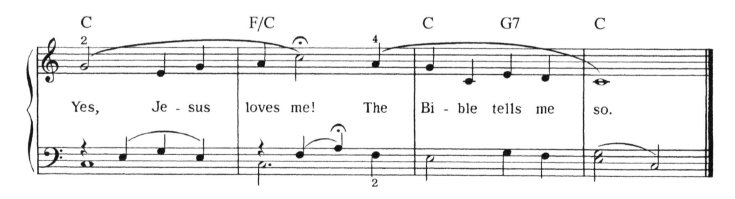

2. Jesus loves me, he who died,
   Heaven's gate to open wide;
   He will wash away my sin,
   Let his little child come in.
   Refrain

3. Jesus loves me, he will stay,
   Close beside me all the way;
   If I love him, when I die
   He will take me home on high.
   Refrain

4. Jesus, take this heart of mine;
   Make it pure, and wholly Thine:
   Thou hast bled and died for me,
   I will henceforth live for Thee.
   Refrain

Just as I Am

Words by Charlotte Elliot
Music by William B. Bradbury

Moderately

1. Just as I am,___ with-out ___ one plea, But that___ Thy

blood was shed for me, And___ that Thou bidd'st___ me come to

Thee,___ O Lamb of God,___ I come, I come.___

2. Just as I am, and waiting not
To rid my soul of one dark blot,
To Thee, whose blood can cleanse each spot,
O Lamb of God, I come, I come.

3. Just as I am, though tossed about
With many a conflict, many a doubt,
Fightings and fears, within, without,
O Lamb of God, I come, I come.

4. Just as I am, poor, wretched, blind,
Sight, riches, healing of the mind,
Yea, all I need, in Thee to find,
O Lamb of God, I come, I come.

5. Just as I am, Thou wilt receive,
Wilt welcome, pardon, cleanse, relieve,
Because Thy promise I believe,
O Lamb of God, I come, I come.

6. Just as I am, Thy love unknown
Hath broken every barrier down;
Now, to be Thine, yea, Thine alone,
O Lamb of God, I come, I come.

The Old Rugged Cross

Words and music by George Bennard

Moderately

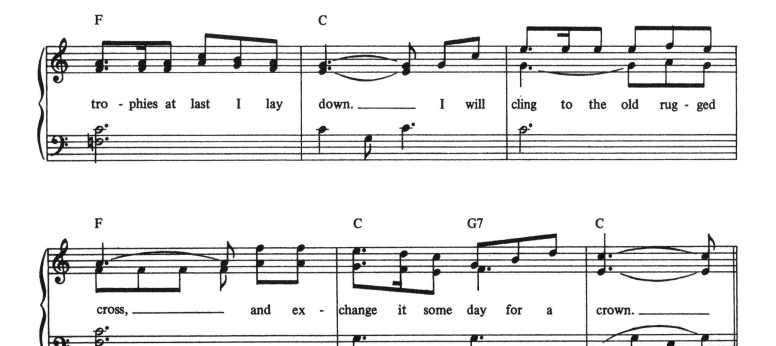

tro - phies at last I lay down. _____ I will cling to the old rug - ged cross, _____ and ex - change it some day for a crown. _____

3. In the old rugged cross, stained with love so divine,
   A wondrous beauty I see;
   For 'twas on that old cross Jesus suffered and died
   To pardon and sanctify me.
   Refrain

4. To the old rugged cross, I will ever be true,
   Its shame and reproach gladly bear;
   Then He'll call me some day to my home far away,
   Where His glory forever I'll share.
   Refrain

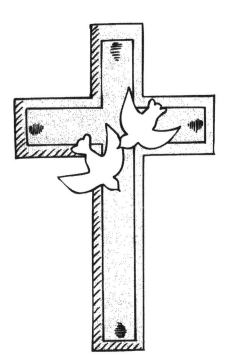

One Sweetly Solemn Thought

Words by Phoebe Cary
Music by Robert S. Ambrose

Quietly

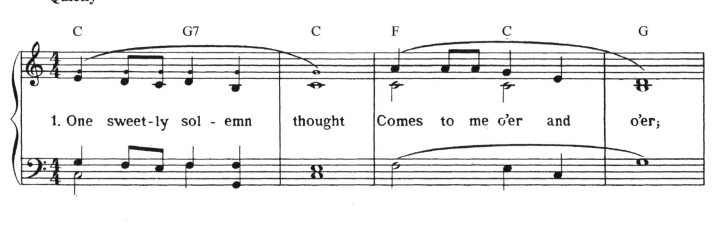

1. One sweet-ly sol - emn thought Comes to me o'er and o'er;

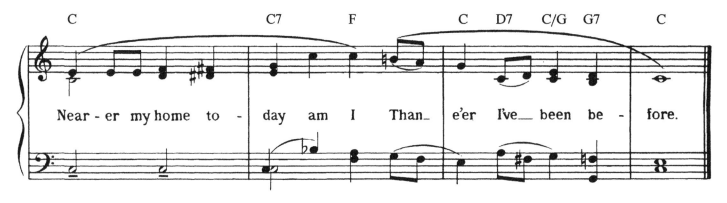

Near - er my home to - day am I Than_ e'er I've_ been be - fore.

2. Nearer my Father's house,
   Where many mansions be;
   Nearer today, the great white throne,
   Nearer the crystal sea.

3. Nearer the bound of life,
   Where burdens are laid down;
   Nearer, to leave the heavy cross,
   Nearer to gain the crown.

4. But, lying dark between,
   Winding down through the night,
   There rolls the deep and unknown stream
   That leads at last to light.

5. Father, perfect my trust!
   Strengthen my pow'r of faith!
   Nor let me stand, at last, alone
   Upon the shore of death.

6. Be Thee near when my feet
   Are slipping over the brink;
   For it may be I'm nearer home,
   Nearer now than I think.

Rock of Ages

Words by Augustus M. Toplady
Music by Thomas Hastings

Moderately

1. Rock of A - ges cleft for me, Let me hide my-self in

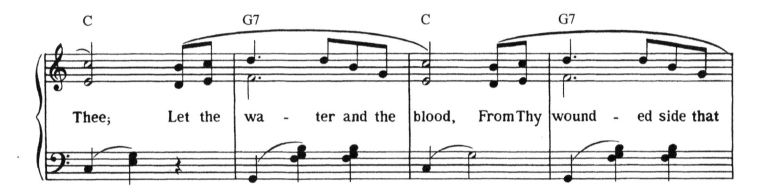

Thee; Let the wa - ter and the blood, From Thy wound - ed side that

flowed, Be of sin the dou-ble cure, Cleanse me from its guilt and pow'r.

2. Could my zeal no respite know,
Could my tears forever flow,
All for sin could not atone,
Thou must save and Thou alone;
Nothing in my hand I bring,
Simply to Thy cross I cling.

3. While I draw this fleeting breath,
When mine eyelids close in death,
When I soar to worlds unknown,
And behold Thee on Thy throne,
Rock of ages, cleft for me,
Let me hide myself in Thee.

Stand Up, Stand Up for Jesus

Words by George Duffield, Jr.
Music by George J. Webb

Moderately

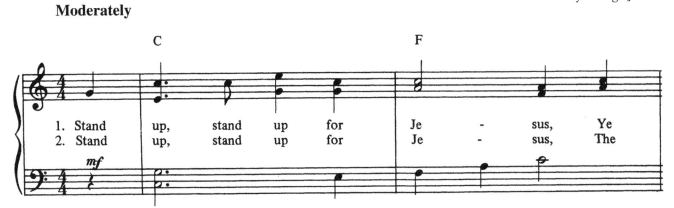

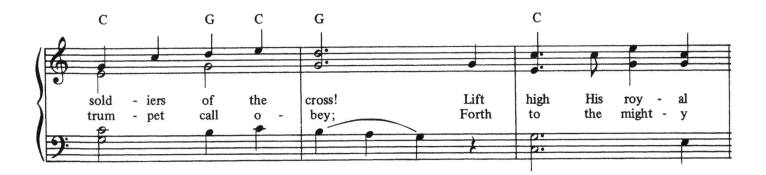

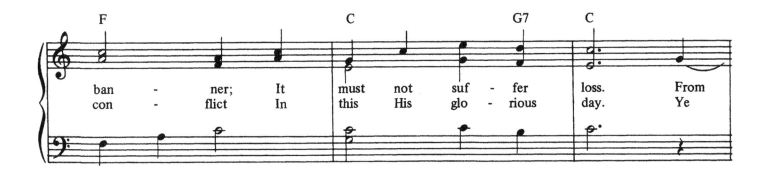

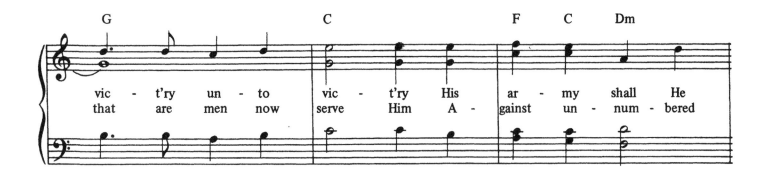

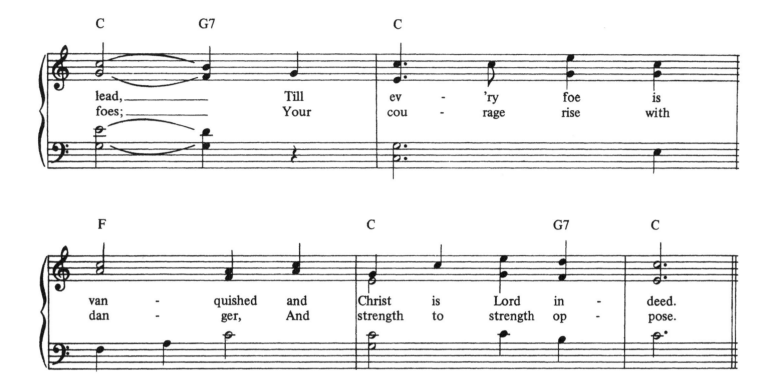

lead,_____ Till ev - 'ry foe is
foes;_____ Your cou - rage rise with

van - quished and Christ is Lord in - deed.
dan - ger, And strength to strength op - pose.

3. Stand up, stand up for Jesus!
Stand in His strength alone;
The arm of flesh will fail you,
Ye dare not trust your own.
Put on the gospel armor,
Each piece put on with prayer:
Where duty calls or danger,
Be never wanting there.

4. Stand up, stand up for Jesus!
Each soldier to his post;
Close up the broken column
And shout through all the host.
Make good the loss so heavy
In those that still remain;
And prove to all around you
That death itself is gain.

5. Stand up, stand up for Jesus!
The strife will not be long;
This day the noise of battle,
The next the victor's song.
To him that overcometh
A crown of life shall be:
He with the King of Glory
Shall reign eternally.

Sweet Hour of Prayer

Words by William W. Walford
Music by William B. Bradbury

Quietly

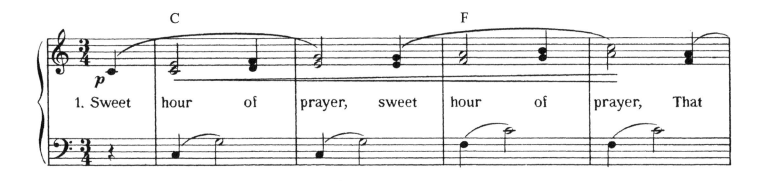

1. Sweet hour of prayer, sweet hour of prayer, That

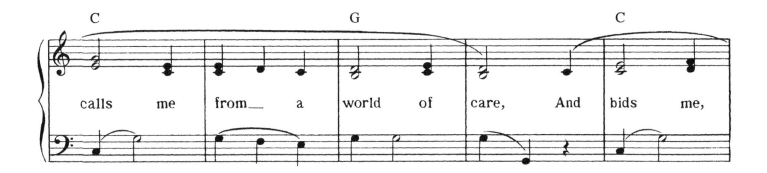

calls me from__ a world of care, And bids me,

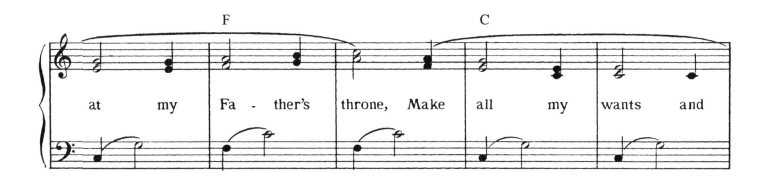

at my Fa-ther's throne, Make all my wants and

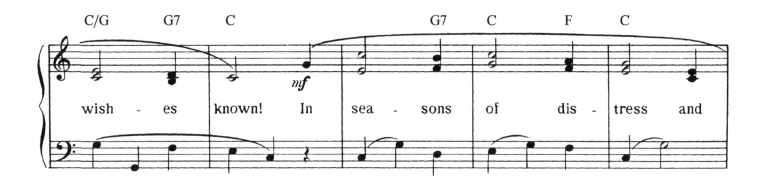

wish - es known! In sea - sons of dis - tress and

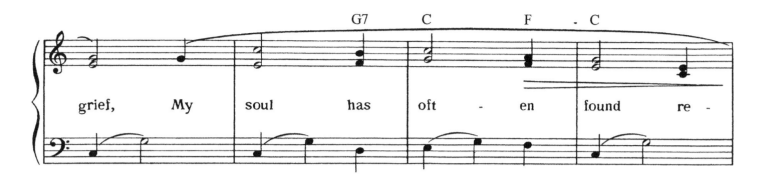

grief, My soul has oft - en found re -

lief; And oft es - caped the tempt - er's

snare By thy re - turn, sweet hour of prayer.

2. Sweet hour of prayer, sweet hour of prayer,
Thy wings shall my petition bear
To Him whose truth and faithfulness
Engage the waiting soul to bless;
And since He bids me seek His face,
Believe His word and trust His grace,
I'll cast on Him my every care
And wait for thee, sweet hour of prayer.

3. Sweet hour of prayer, sweet hour of prayer,
May I thy consolation share,
Till from Mount Pisgah's lofty height
I view my home and take my flight;
In my immortal flesh I'll rise
To seize the everlasting prize,
And shout while passing through the air,
Farewell, farewell, sweet hour of prayer!

Shall We Gather at the River?

Words and music by Robert Lowry

Moderately

1. Shall we gath-er at the riv - er, Where bright an-gel feet have trod;__ With its crys-tal tide for - ev - er Flow-ing from the throne of__ God?
2. On the mar-gin of the riv - er, Wash-ing up its sil - ver spray,__ We shall walk and wor-ship ev - er All the hap-py, gold-en__ day.

REFRAIN

Yes, we'll gath-er at the riv - er, The beau-ti-ful, the beau-ti-ful__ riv - er, Gath-er with the saints__ at the riv - er, That flows from the throne of__ God.

3. Ere we reach the shining river,
   Lay we every burden down;
   Grace our spirits will deliver,
   And provide a robe and crown.
   Refrain

4. Soon we'll reach the silver river,
   Soon our pilgrimage will cease;
   Soon our happy hearts will quiver
   With the melody of peace.
   Refrain

Tell Me Why

American folk song

Slowly

212

There Is a Happy Land

Words by Andrew Young
Music by Leonard P. Breedlove

Moderately

mf 1. There is a happy land, Far, far a-way, Where saints in glo-ry stand, Bright, bright as day;

f Oh, how they sweetly sing, Worthy is our Savior King, Loud let His praises ring, Praise, praise for aye!

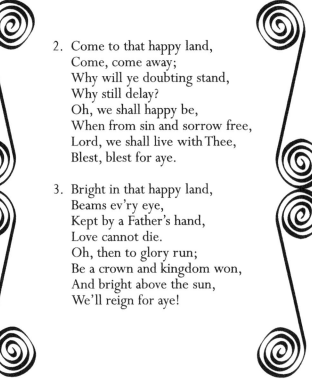

2. Come to that happy land,
   Come, come away;
   Why will ye doubting stand,
   Why still delay?
   Oh, we shall happy be,
   When from sin and sorrow free,
   Lord, we shall live with Thee,
   Blest, blest for aye.

3. Bright in that happy land,
   Beams ev'ry eye,
   Kept by a Father's hand,
   Love cannot die.
   Oh, then to glory run;
   Be a crown and kingdom won,
   And bright above the sun,
   We'll reign for aye!

What a Friend We Have in Jesus

Words by Joseph Scriven
Music by Charles C. Converse

3. Are we weak and heavy-laden,
Cumbered with a load of care?
Precious Savior, still our refuge,
Take it to the Lord in prayer!
Do thy friends despise, forsake thee?
Take it to the Lord in prayer!
In His arms He'll take and shield thee,

Whispering Hope

Words and music by Alice Hawthorne

Moderately slow

mp

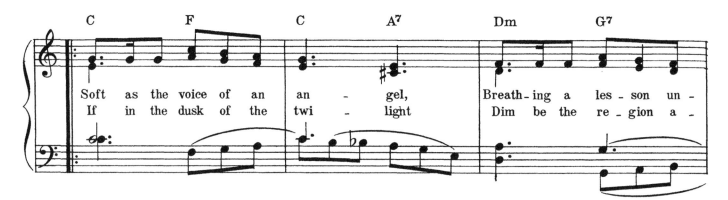

Soft as the voice of an an — gel, Breath — ing a les — son un —
If in the dusk of the twi — light Dim be the re — gion a —

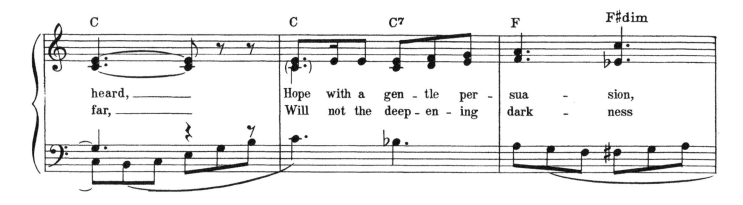

heard, _____ Hope with a gen — tle per — sua — sion,
far, _____ Will not the deep — en — ing dark — ness

Whis — pers her com — fort — ing word: _____ Wait, till the dark — ness is
Bright — en the glim — mer — ing star? _____ Then, when the night is up —

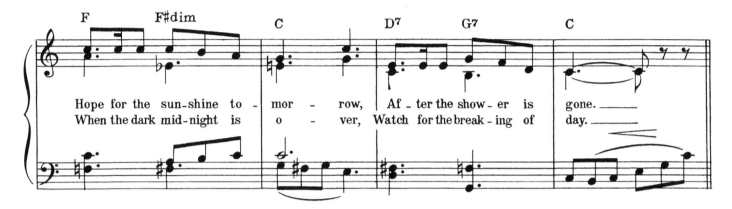

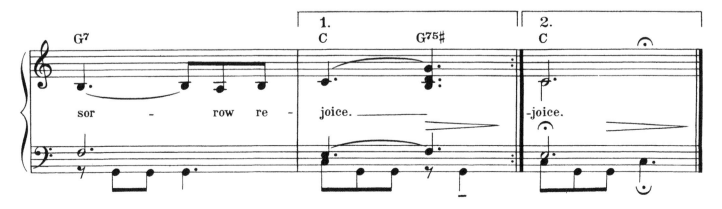

SACRED CLASSICS

Jesu, Joy of Man's Desiring

Johann Sebastian Bach

Andantino

Je - su,   Joy   of
Drawn by Thee of   our

man's   de - sir - ing,
souls   as - pir - ing

Ho - ly
Soar to

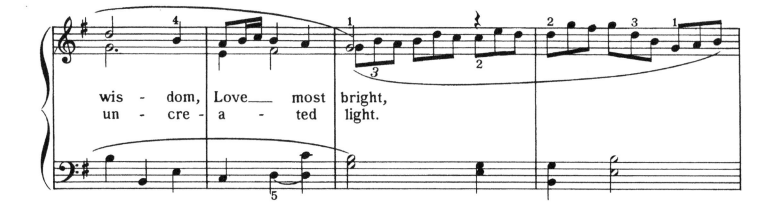

wis - dom, Love___ most bright,
un - cre - a - ted light.

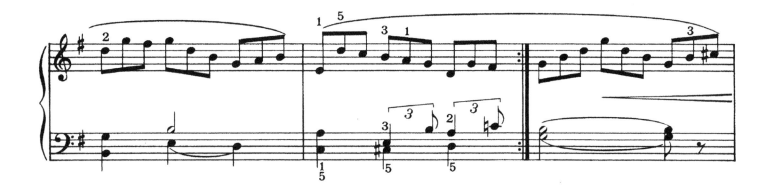

Word of God, our flesh___ that fash - ioned

220

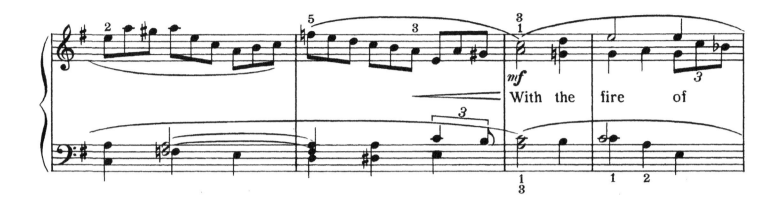

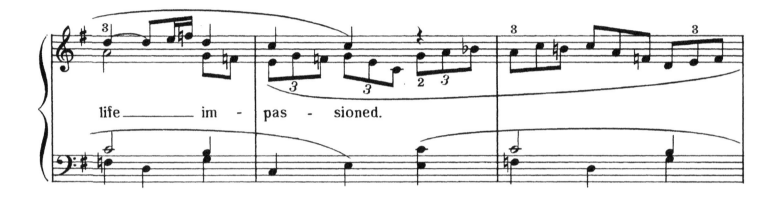

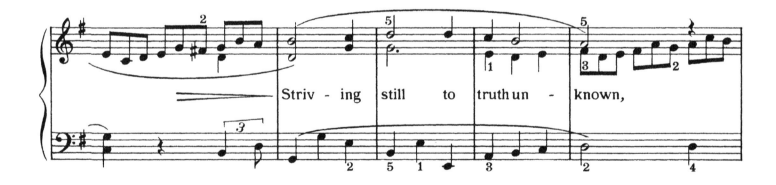

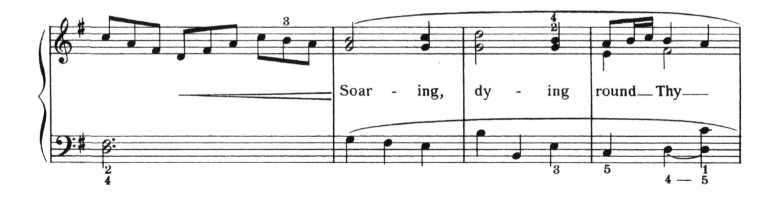

throne.

My Heart Ever Faithful

Johann Sebastian Bach

Andante con moto

mf

p

My

heart_____ ev - er   faith - ful, Sing   prais - es, be

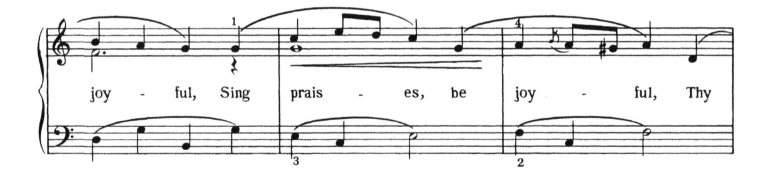

joy - ful, Sing   prais - es, be   joy - ful, Thy

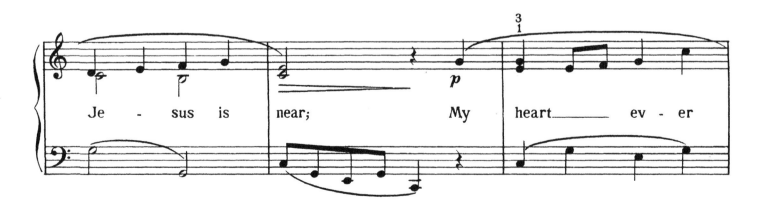

Je - sus is   near;   My   heart_____ ev - er

faith - ful, Sing prais - es, be joy - ful, Sing

prais - es, be joy - ful, Thy Je - sus is

near!

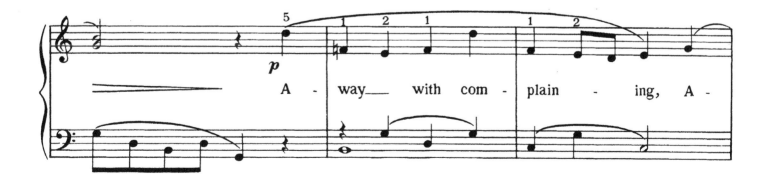

A - way___ with com - plain - ing, A -

224

way___ with com - plain - ing, Faith ev - er main -

tain - ing, My Je - sus is here; A -

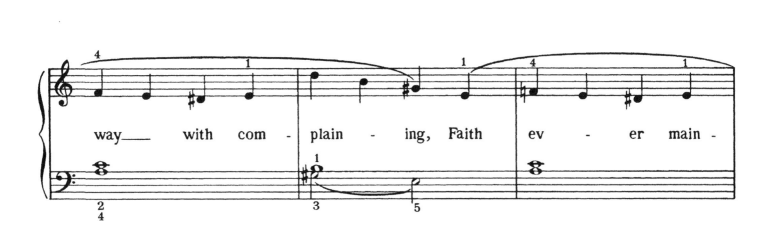

way___ with com - plain - ing, Faith ev - er main -

tain - ing, My Je - sus is here, My___

Je - sus is here. My heart___ ev - er faith - ful, Sing

prais - es, be joy - ful, Sing prais - es, be

joy - ful, Thy___ Je - sus is here;

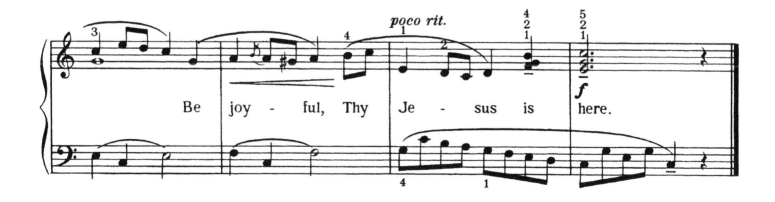

Be joy - ful, Thy Je - sus is here.

Prepare Thyself, Zion

from *Christmas Oratorio*

Johann Sebastian Bach

With movement

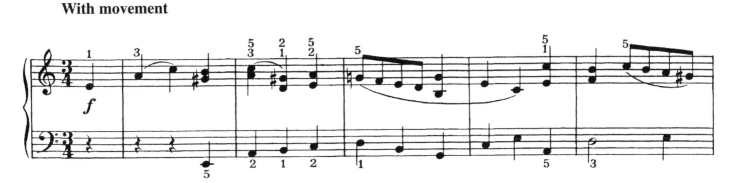

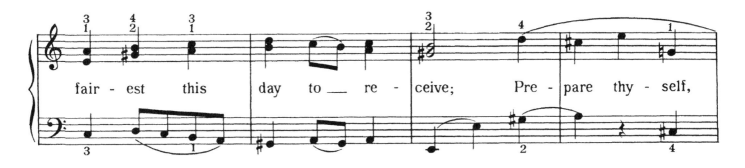

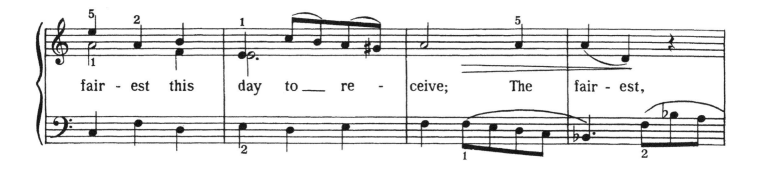

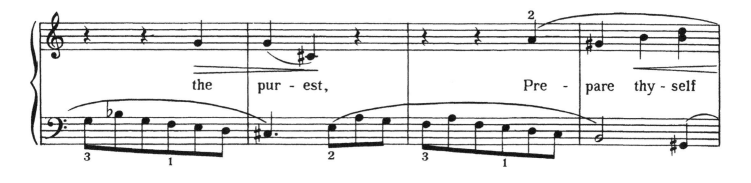

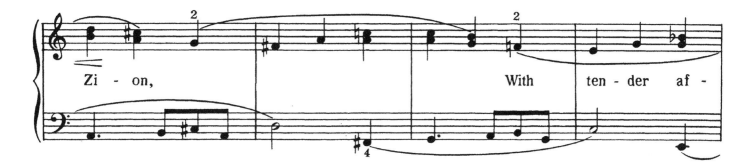

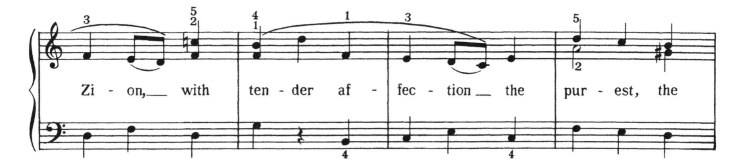

fair - est this day to re - ceive._____ *Fine* Thou must

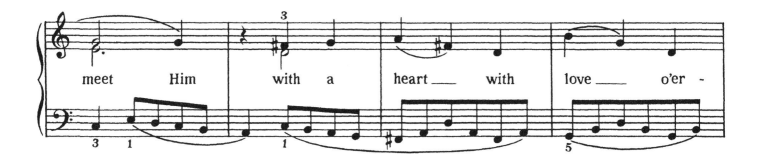

meet Him with a heart ___ with love ___ o'er -

flow - ing, *cresc.* With a heart ___ with love ___ o'er -

flow - ing, *mf* Haste then, with ar - dour the Bride - groom to

wel - come. *mp* *f* Pre-

D. S. 𝄋

Ave Maria

Johann Sebastian Bach & Charles Gounod

Andante

con Ped.

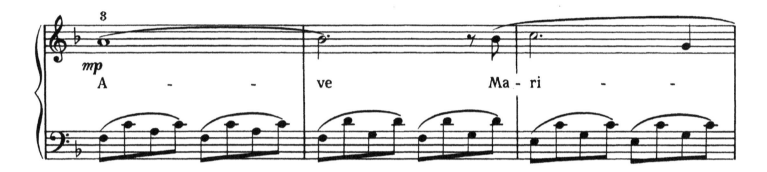

A - ve Ma - ri - -

a, Thou_____ high-ly fa - vored,

God _____ is___ with_____ thee. Bless - ed,___

230

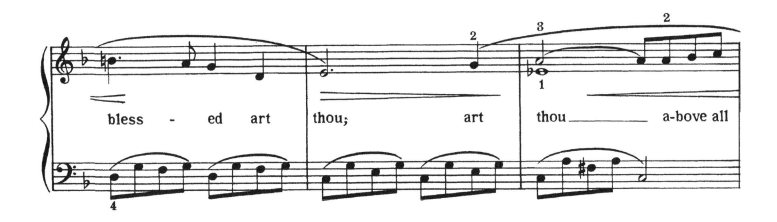

bless - ed art thou; art thou_____ a-bove all

wo - men, Bless - ed be thine off - spring,

cresc.

Bless - ed be thy Son,_____ the Son of God, the Lord most high!

mf

Bless - ed Ma - ri - a! Bless - ed Ma-

cresc. poco a poco

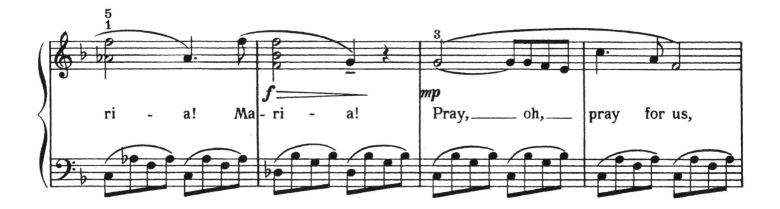

ri - a! Ma - ri - a! Pray,___ oh,___ pray for us,

pray___ for us, poor sin - ners, Now___ and when the

hour___ of our death,___ our_ death_ o'er_ takes_ us.___

A - men! A - men!

Agnus Dei
(Lamb of God)

Georges Bizet

Maestoso

Andantino

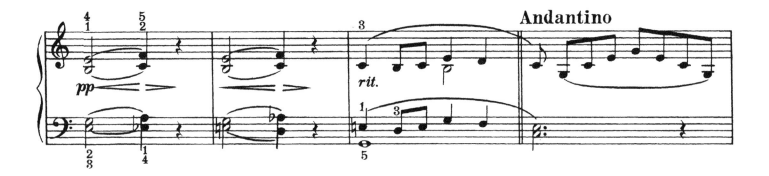

A - - gnus De - i! Qui tol - lis pec-ca - ta
Lamb___ of God, Thou that tak - est a - way the

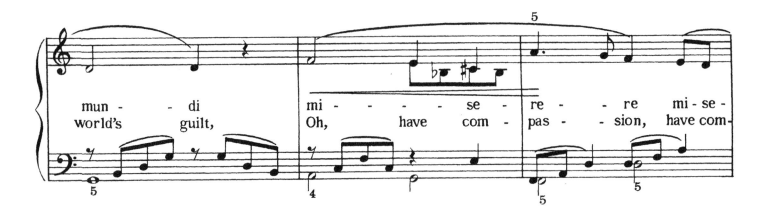

mun - di
world's guilt,

mi - - se - re - re mi-se-
Oh, have com - pas - sion, have com-

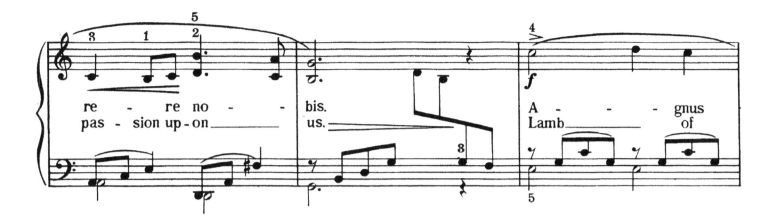

re - re no - - bis.
pas - sion up-on_____ us._____ A - gnus of
Lamb_____ of

De - - i! Qui tol - lis pec-ca - ta mun - di,
God,_____ thou that tak - est a - way___ the world's___ guilt,

mi - se - re - re, mi - se - re - re, mi - se - re - re
Have com-pas - sion, have com-pas - sion, have com-pas - sion up-

no - - bis. A - gnus, A - gnus De - - i! Qui
on us. Lamb of God, Lamb of God,_____ Thou that

tol - lis pec - ca - ta mun - di,
tak - est a - way the world's guilt,

A - gnus De - i! Qui
Lamb of God, Thou that

cresc. molto

tol - lis pec - ca - ta mun - di, do - na
tak - est a - way the world's guilt, may Thy

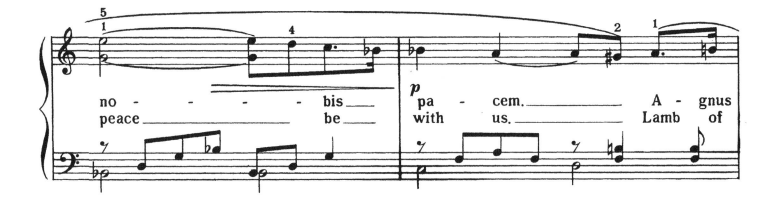

no - - - bis pa - cem. A - gnus
peace be with us. Lamb of

Allargando

De - i!_____ Do - na pa - cem. A - gnus De - i! Do - na
God,_____ may Thy peace, Thy peace be with us, may Thy

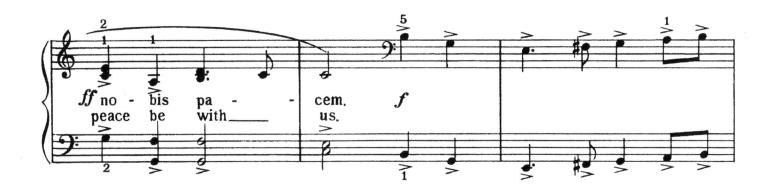

no - bis pa - - cem.
peace be with___ us.

Do - na
Thy peace,

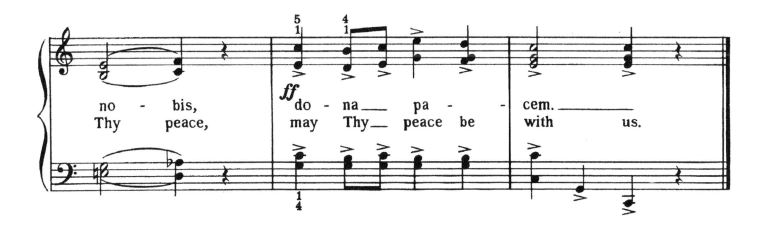

no - bis, do - na___ pa - - cem._____
Thy peace, may Thy__ peace be with____ us.

The Palms

Jean Baptiste Faure

Moderately slow

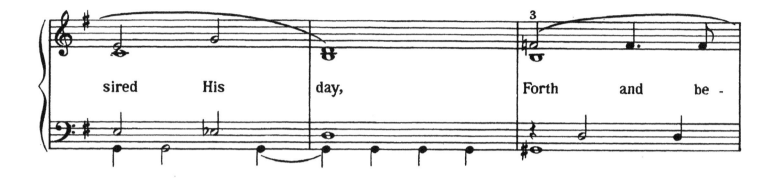

sired His day, Forth and be -

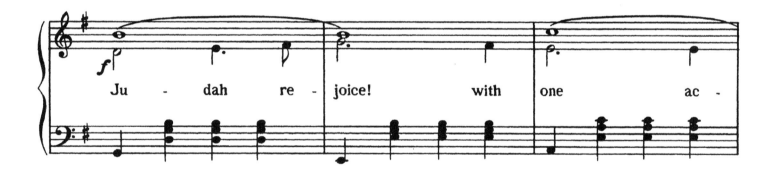

hold Him on this fes - tal morn!

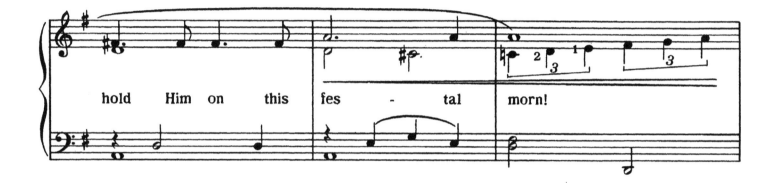

Ju - dah re - joice! with one ac -

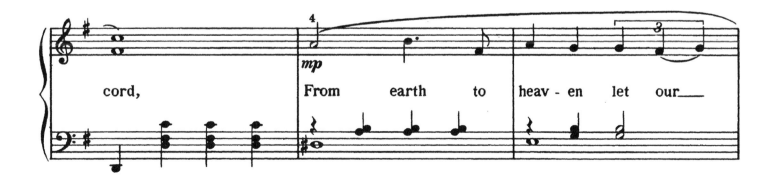

cord, From earth to heav - en let our

voi - - ces wave,_____ Ho - san - -

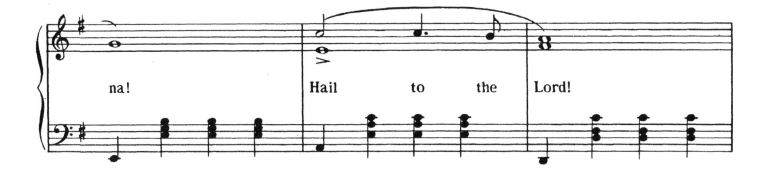

na! Hail to the Lord!

Allargando

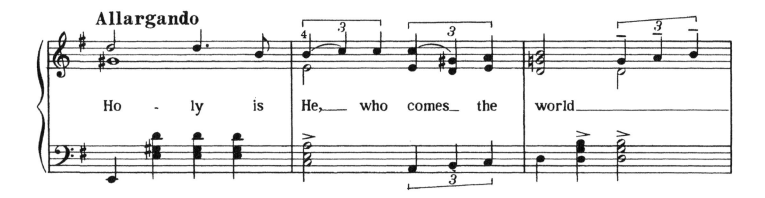

Ho - ly is He,___ who comes_ the world_____

_____ to save!

Panis Angelicus
(O Lord of Mercy)

Words by Michel Whitehill
Music by César Franck

Andante

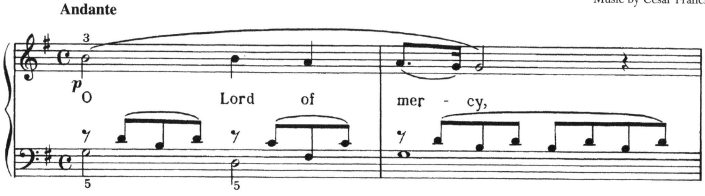

O Lord of mer - cy,

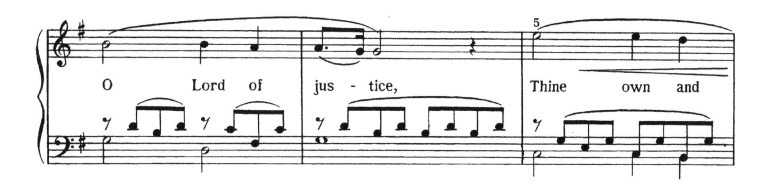

O Lord of jus - tice, Thine own and

hum - ble ser - vants seek to find re - demp - tion.

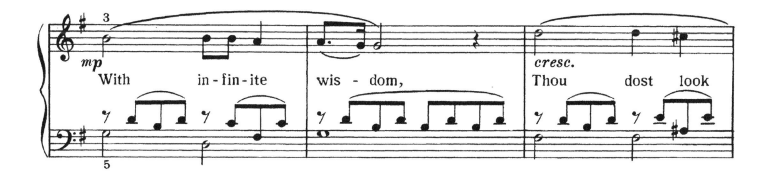

With in - fin - ite wis - dom, Thou dost look

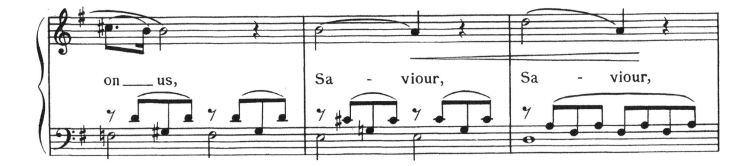

on ____ us,   Sa - viour,   Sa - viour,

Thou art mi - rac - u - lous;   Sa - viour,

Sa - viour,   we would Thy ser - vants be.

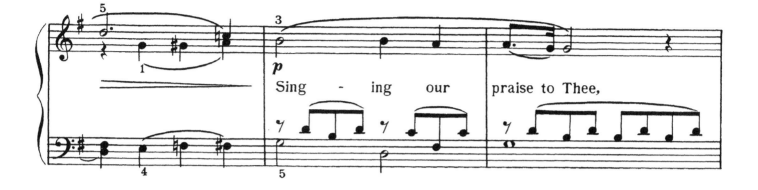

Sing - ing our praise to Thee,

To Thee our hearts flee, Glo - rious Thy

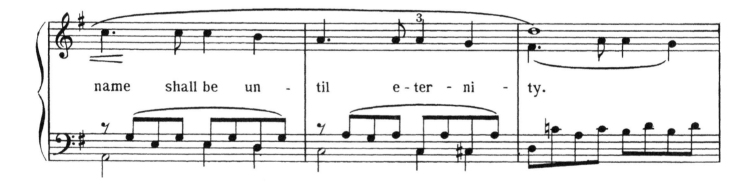

name shall be un - til e - ter - ni - ty.

E'en in the si - lent night Thy glo - ry

shin - ing bright, *mf* Pro - - - - claims to

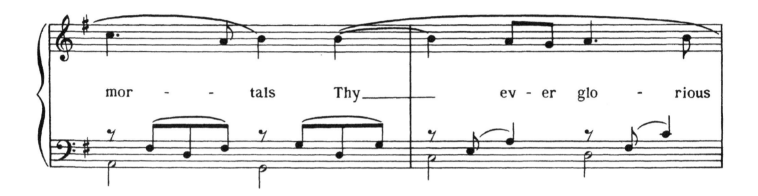

mor - - tals Thy___ ev - er glo - rious

might; *f* Fath - - er___ of___ men to___

dim. The_ we bring our song,___ of praise.

Hallelujah Chorus

from *Messiah*

George Frideric Handel

Allegro moderato

f Hal - le-lu-jah! Hal - le-lu-jah! Hal-le-lu-jah! Hal-le-lu-jah! Hal

le - lu-jah! Hal - le-lu-jah! Hal - le-lu-jah! Hal-le-

lu-jah! Hal-le-lu-jah! Hal - le - lu - jah! For the Lord

God om-ni - po-tent reign - eth. Hal-le - lu-jah! Hal-le-lu-jah! Hal-le-

lu - jah! Hal-le-lu-jah! For the Lord God om - ni - po - tent

reign - eth. Hal-le - lu - jah! Hal-le-lu-jah! Hal-le - lu - jah! Hal-le-lu-jah!

For the Lord God om - ni - po - tent reign - eth. Hal-le -

lu - jah! Hal - le - lu - jah! Hal - le - lu - jah! Hal - le - lu - jah!

And He shall reign for - ev - er and ev - er. And He shall reign for -

ev - er and ev - er. And He shall reign for-ev - er and

ev - er, shall reign for-ev - er, for-ev - er and ev -

er. Hal-le-lu-jah! Hal-le-lu-jah! Hal-le-lu-jah! Hal-le-

lu-jah! *ff* Hal - le - lu - jah!

He Shall Feed His Flock

from *Messiah*

George Frideric Handel

Lento

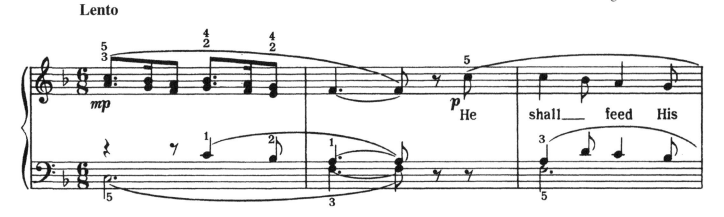

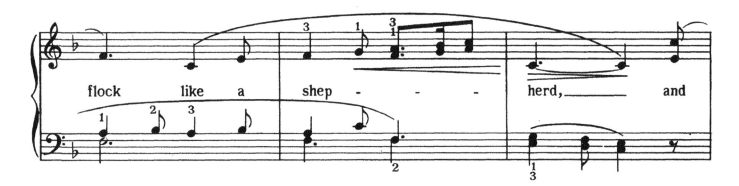

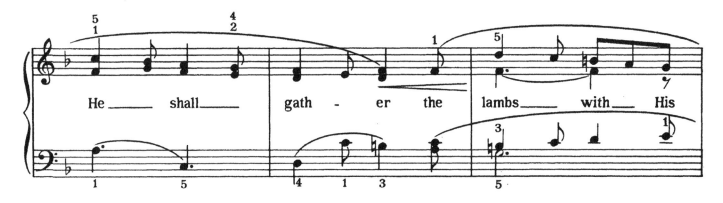

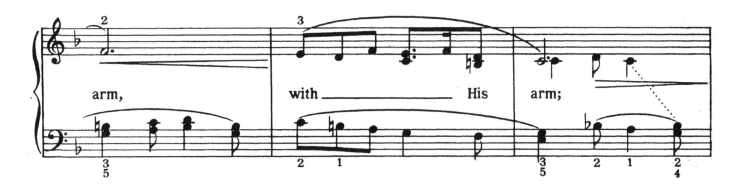

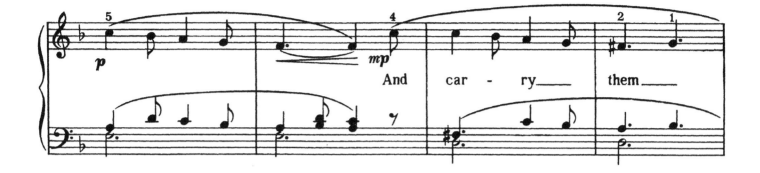

And car - ry___ them___

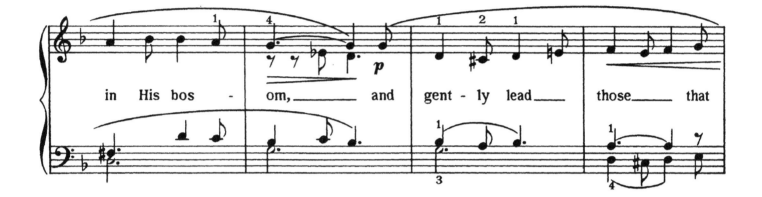

in His bos - om,___ and gent - ly lead___ those___ that

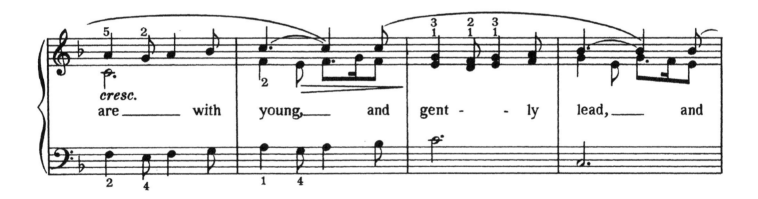

are___ with young,___ and gent - ly lead,___ and

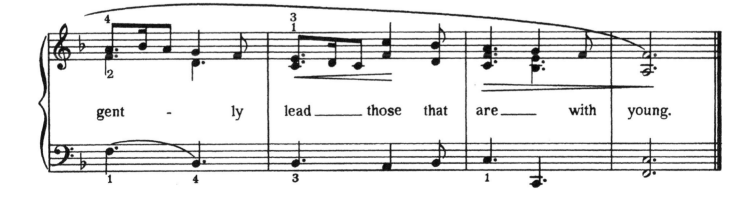

gent - ly lead___ those that are___ with young.

O Thou Who Dryest the Mourner's Tear

Words by Thomas Moore
Music by Franz Joseph Haydn

Larghetto

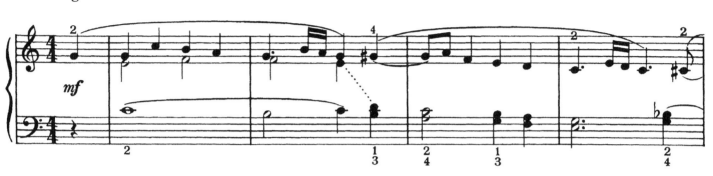

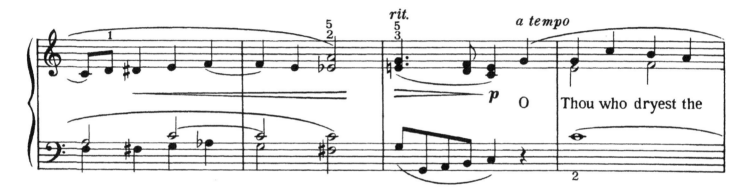

O Thou who dryest the mourn-er's tear, How dark__ this world would be,_____ If, when de-ceiv'd and

wound - ed here, We could not fly to Thee._____ The friends who in our

sun-shine   live,   When   win - ter comes, are   flown;   And

he   who has but   tears to give, Must weep those tears a - lone.   But

Thou wilt heal that   bro-ken heart, Which, like___ the plants that   throw___ Their

fra-grance from the   wound-ed part, Breathes sweet-ness out___ of   woe.___

I Know That My Redeemer Liveth

from *Messiah*

George Frideric Handel

Larghetto

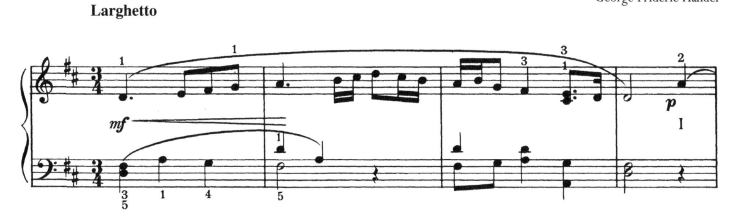

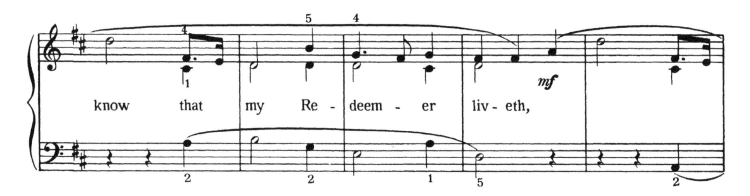

know that my Re - deem - er liv - eth,

And that He shall stand_____

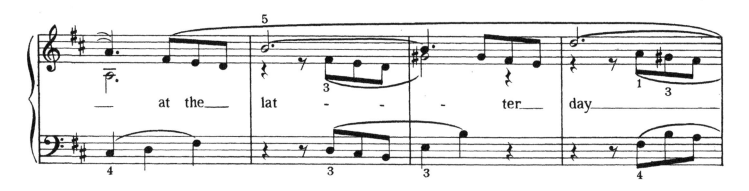

_____ at the___ lat - - - ter___ day___

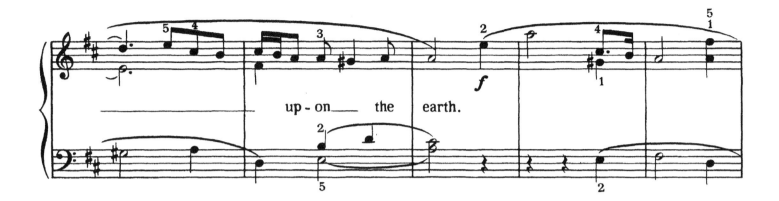

up - on___ the earth.

I know that___ my Re - deem - er

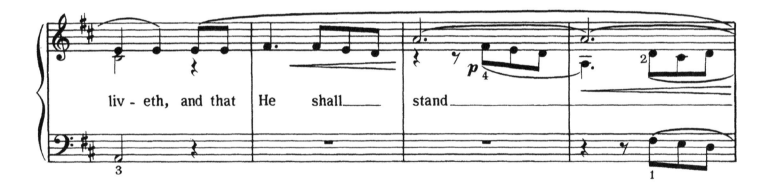

liv - eth, and that He shall___ stand___

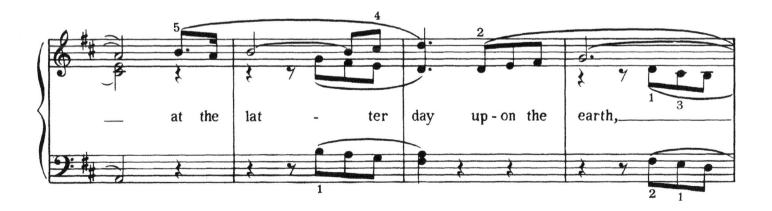

___ at the lat - ter day up - on the earth,___

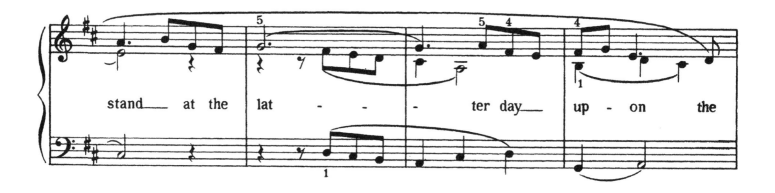

Brightest and Best

Words by Reginald Heber
Music by Felix Mendelssohn

Moderately slow

1. Bright-est and best of the sons of the
2. Cold on His cra-dle the dewdrops are

morn-ing! Dawn on our dark-ness, and lend us thine aid! Star of the East — the ho - ri - zon a -
shin-ing Low lies His head with the beasts of the stall; An-gels a - dore Him, in slum-ber re -

dorn-ing, Guide where our In-fant Re-deemer is laid!
clin-ing, Ma - ker and Mon - arch, Sav-ior of all!

3. Say, shall we yield Him, in costly devotion,
   Odors of Edom, and off'rings divine,
   Gems of the mountain, and pearls of the ocean,
   Myrrh from the forest and gold from the mine?

4. Vainly we offer each ample oblation,
   Vainly with gifts would His favor secure;
   Richer, by far, is the heart's adoration,
   Dearer to God are the prayers of the poor.

But the Lord Is Mindful

from *St. Paul*

Felix Mendelssohn

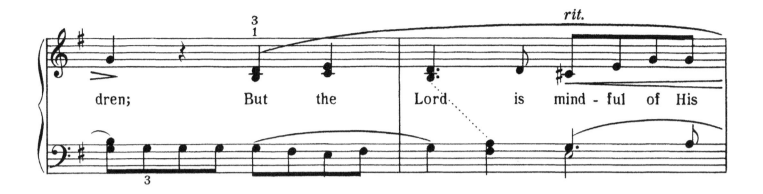

dren; But the Lord is mind - ful of His

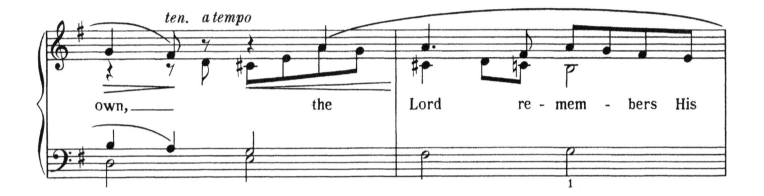

own, ___ the Lord re - mem - bers His

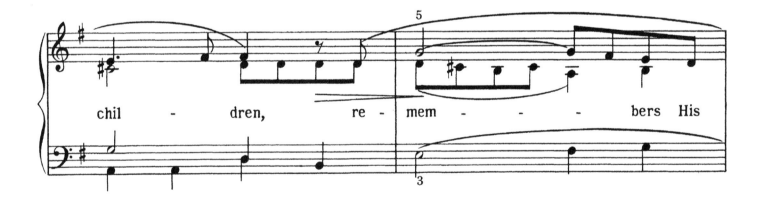

chil - dren, re - mem - - - bers His

chil - dren.

256

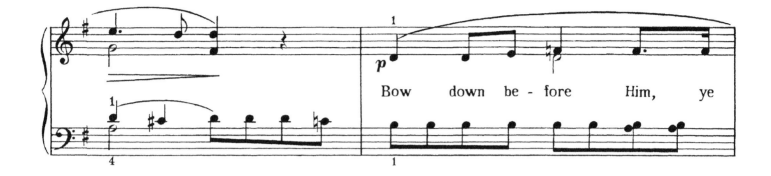

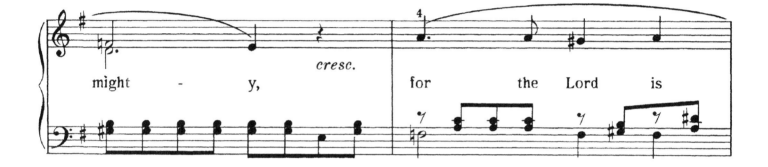

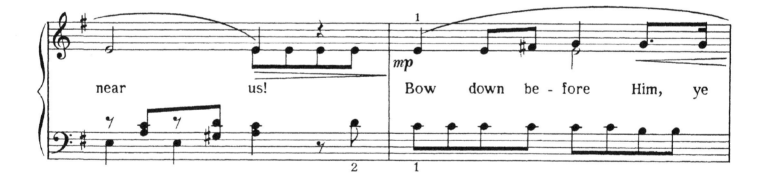

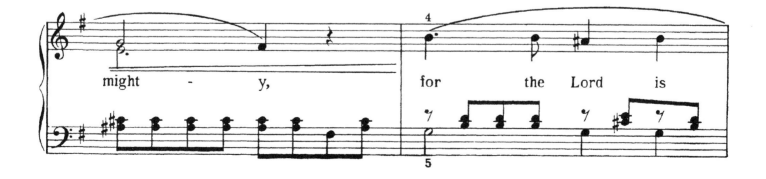

near ... us! Yea, the Lord is mind-ful of His own;— He re - mem - bers His chil -

dren; Bow down be - fore Him, ye might - y, for the

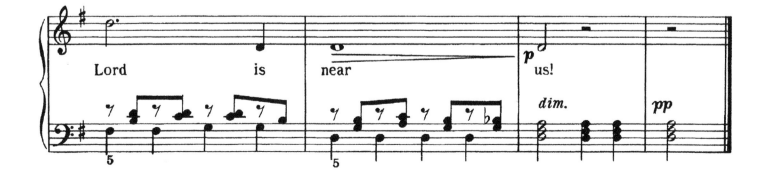

Lord is near us!

Bridal Chorus

from *Lohengrin*

Richard Wagner

Slowly

Faith-ful and true we lead you forth, Where love tri-

um-phant shall crown you with joy! Star of re-nown, flow'r of the earth, Blest be ye

both far from all life's an - noy. -noy. Cham-pion vic - to-rious, go thou be-

fore! Maid bright and glo-rious, go thou be - fore! Mirth's noi - sy re - vel,

you've for - sa - ken, ten-der de - lights for you now a - wa - ken! Fra-grant a-

bode en - shrine you in bliss, Splen-dor and state in joy you dis - miss.

D. S. al Fine

Alleluja

Wolfgang Amadeus Mozart

Allegro

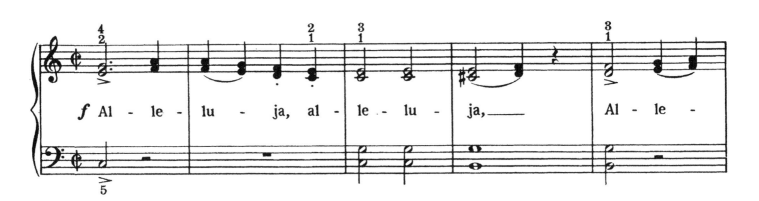

f Al - le - lu - ja, al - le - lu - ja,____ Al - le -

lu - ja, al - le - lu - ja! Al - le - lu - ja, al -

le - lu - ja,____ Al - le - lu - ja, al - le - lu -

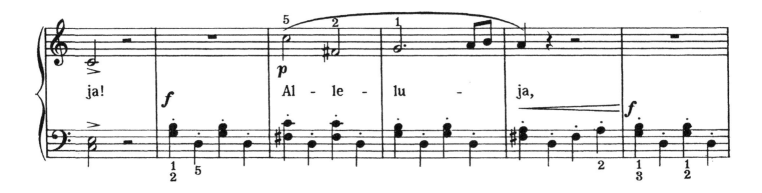

ja! Al - le - lu - ja,____

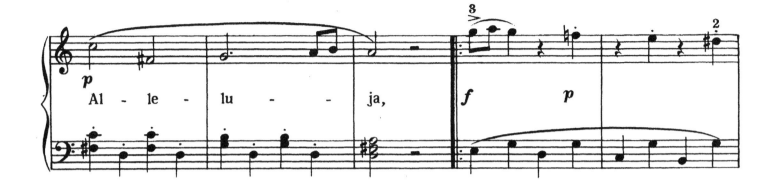

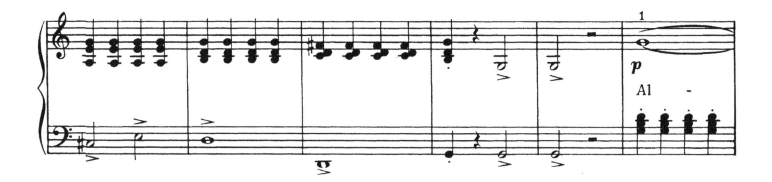

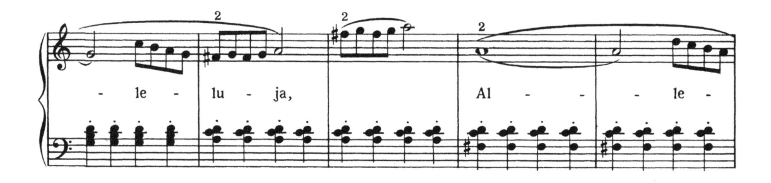

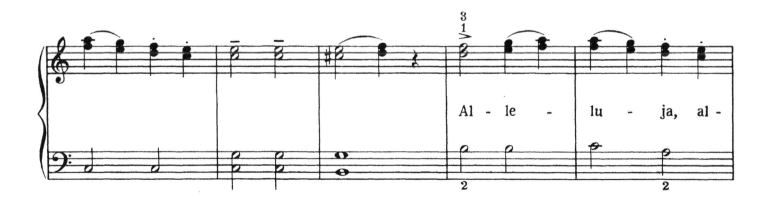

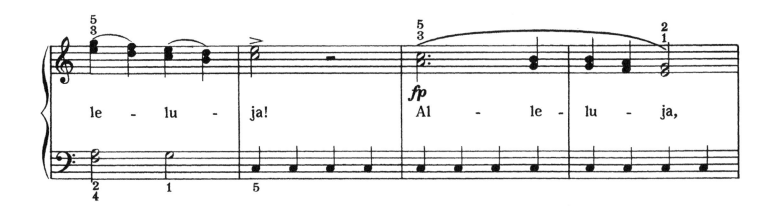

le - lu - ja! Al - le - lu - ja,

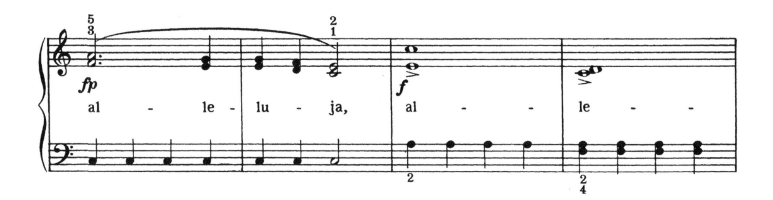

al - le - lu - ja, al - le -

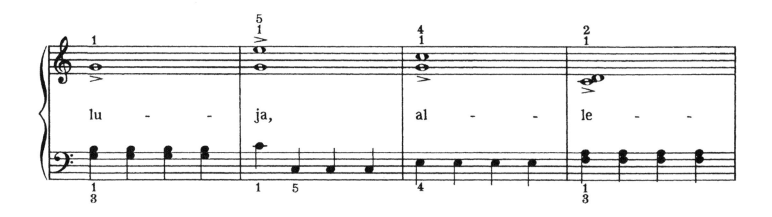

lu - ja, al - le -

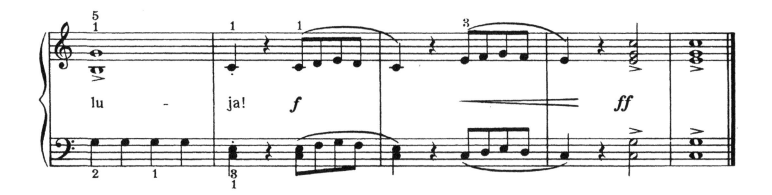

lu - ja!

Ave Maria

Franz Schubert

Lento

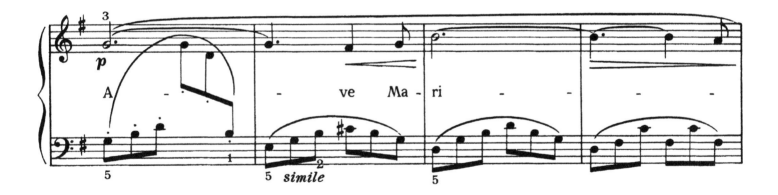

266

na,_____ Ma - ri - a,__ gra - ti - a
mild,_____ Ah, lis - ten__ to a maid - en's

ple - na,_____ Ma - ri - a, gra - ti - a __ ple-
prayer;_____ For Thou_____ canst hear__ a - mid__ the

na, _____ A - ve,_____ A - ve, Do - mi-
wild,_____ 'Tis__ Thou,_____ 'tis Thou canst save__ a-

nus,_____ Do-mi - nus__ te - cum._____ Ben - e-
mid_____ de - spair._____ We__

di - cta tu in mu - li - e - ri - bus,_____ et
slum - ber safe - ly till the mor - row,_____ Tho'

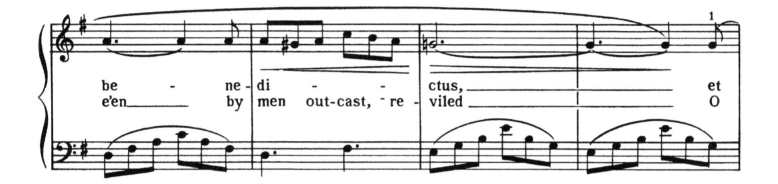

be - ne - di - ctus,_____ et
e'en_____ by men out-cast, re - viled_____ O

be - ne - di - ctus fru - ctus ven - tris,_____
Maid - - en, see a maid - en's sor - row,_____

_____ ven-tris tu - i, Je - sus._____
_____ O Moth - er, hear a sup-pliant child!_____

267

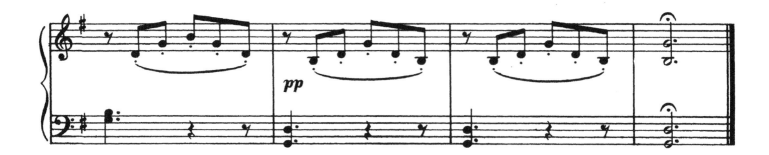

HOME FOR THE HOLIDAYS

Christ the Lord Is Risen Today

Easter Carol

Words by Charles Wesley
Medieval carol

Moderately

2. Vain the stone, the watch, the seal; Alleluia!
Christ has burst the gates of hell: Alleluia!
Death in vain forbids His rise, Alleluia!
Christ hath opened Paradise; Alleluia!

3. Soar we now where Christ hath led; Alleluia!
Following our exalted Head; Alleluia!
Made like Him, like Him we rise, Alleluia!
Ours the cross, the grave, the skies; Alleluia!

There Is a Green Hill Far Away

Easter Carol

Words by Cecil Frances Alexander
Music by George C. Stebbins

Moderately fast

1. There is a green hill far a - way, With out a ci - ty
2. We may not know, we can - not tell, What pains He had to

wall, Where the dear Lord was cru - ci - fied, Who died to save us all.
bear, But we be - lieve it was for us He hung and suf - fered there.

3. He died that we might be forgiven,
   He died to make us good;
   That we might go at last to heaven,
   Saved by His precious blood.

4. There was no other good enough
   To pay the price of sin:
   He only could unlock the gate
   Of Heaven, and let us in.

5. O dearly, dearly has He loved,
   And we must love Him too,
   And trust in His redeeming blood,
   And try His works to do.

Were You There

American spiritual

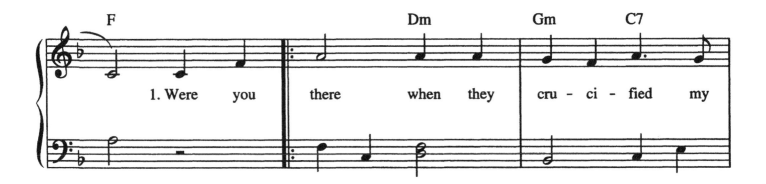

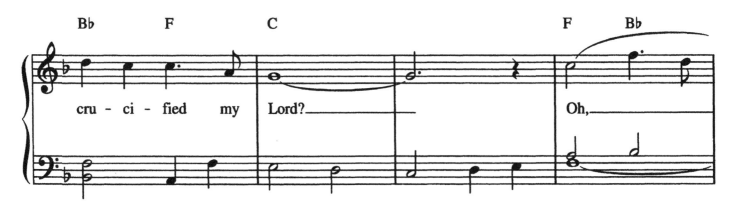

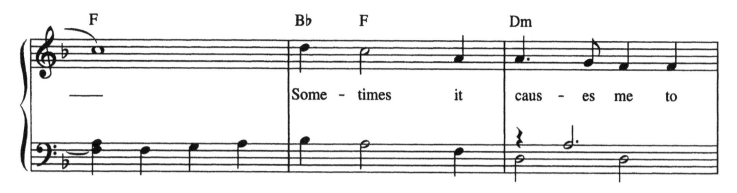

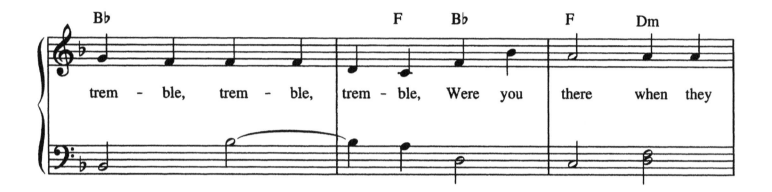

— Some - times it caus - es me to

trem - ble, trem - ble, trem - ble, Were you there when they

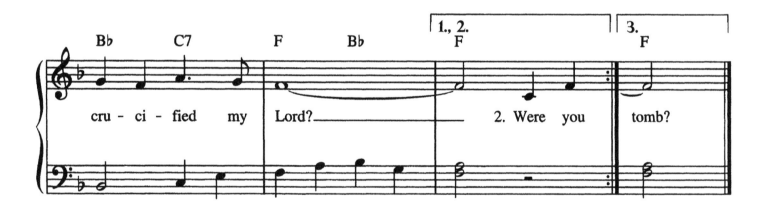

cru - ci - fied my Lord?_____ 2. Were you tomb?

2. Were you there when they nailed him to the tree?
   Were you there when they nailed him to the tree?
   Oh, sometimes it causes me to tremble, tremble, tremble,
   Were you there when they nailed him to the tree?

3. Were you there when they laid him in the tomb?
   Were you there when they laid him in the tomb?
   Oh, sometimes it causes me to tremble, tremble, tremble,
   Were you there when they laid him in the tomb?

Come, Ye Thankful People, Come

Words by Henry Alford
Music by George J. Elvey

Moderately

2. All the world is God's own field,
Fruit unto his praise to yield;
Wheat and tares together sown,
Unto joy or sorrow grown;
First the blade, and then the ear,
Then the full corn shall appear;
Lord of harvest, grant that we
Wholesome grain and pure may be.

3. For the Lord our God shall come,
Bring thy final harvest home;
Gather thou thy people in,
Free from sorrow, free from sin,
There, forever purified,
In thy presence to abide;
Come, with all thine angels, come,
Raise the gorious harvest home.

Prayer of Thanksgiving
(We Gather Together)

Netherlands hymn

Moderately fast

2. Beside us to guide us, our God with us joining,
   Ordaining, maintaining His kingdom divine,
   So from the beginning the fight we were winning;
   Thou, Lord, wast at our side, all glory be Thine.

3. We all do extol Thee, Thou Leader triumphant,
   And pray that Thou still our defender wilt be.
   Let Thy congregation escape tribulation!
   Thy name be ever praised! O Lord, make us free!

We Plough the Fields and Scatter

Words by Matthias Claudius
Music by Johann Abraham Peter Schülz

Moderately

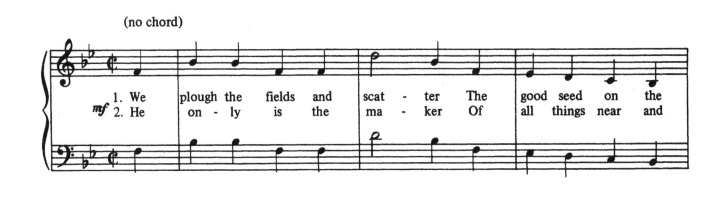

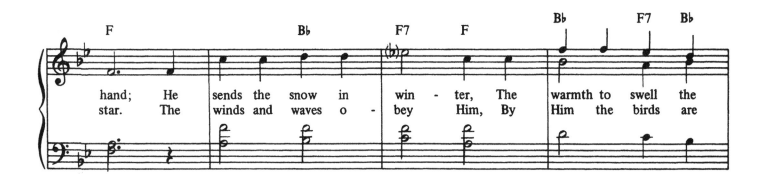

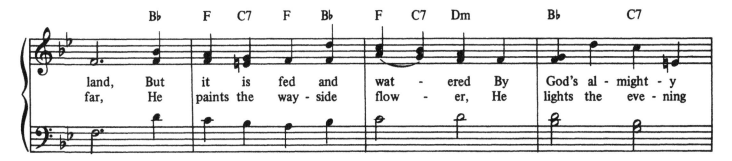

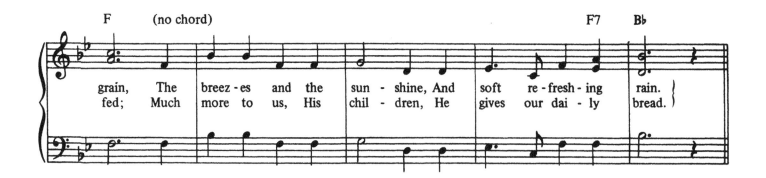

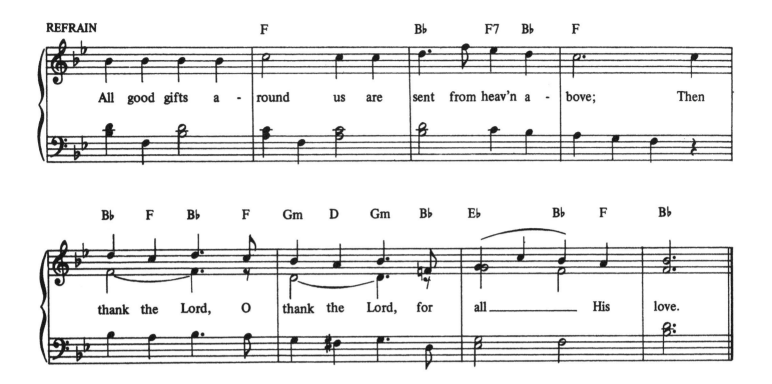

REFRAIN

All good gifts a - round us are sent from heav'n a - bove; Then thank the Lord, O thank the Lord, for all _____ His love.

3. We thank Thee then, O Father,
   For all things bright and good:
   The seed-time and the harvest,
   Our life, our health, our food.
   No gifts have we to offer
   For all Thy love imparts,
   But that which Thou desirest,
   Our humble, thankful hearts.
   Refrain

All My Heart This Night Rejoices

Words by C. Winkworth
Music by J.C. Eberling

3. Come then, let us hasten yonder;
   Here let all,
   Great and small,
   Kneel in awe and wonder;
   Love Him who with love is yearning;
   Hail the star
   That from far
   Bright with hope is burning.

4. Blessed Savior, let me find Thee,
   Keep Thou me,
   Close to Thee,
   Cast me not behind Thee:
   Life of life, my heart Thou stillest,
   Calm I rest
   On Thy breast,
   All this void Thou fillest.

Angels from the Realms of Glory

Words by James Montgomery
Music by Henry Smart

With spirit

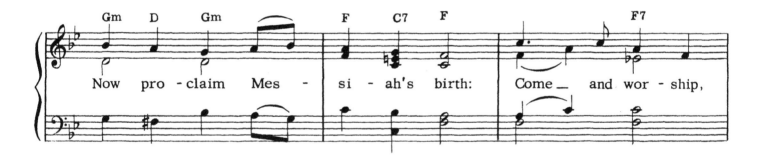

2. Shepherds, in the fields abiding,
Watching o'er your flocks by night,
God with man is now residing,
Yonder shines the infant Light:
Come and worship, Come and worship,
Worship Christ, the newborn King!

3. Sages, leave your contemplations,
Brighter visions beam afar;
Seek the great Desire of nations;
Ye have seen His natal star:
Come and worship, Come and worship,
Worship Christ, the newborn King!

Angels We Have Heard on High

French carol

Moderately

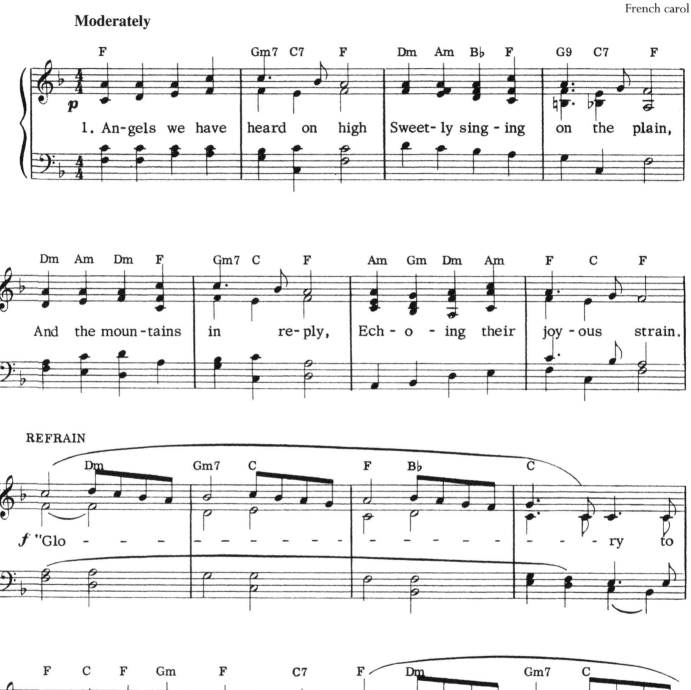

1. An-gels we have heard on high Sweet-ly sing-ing on the plain,

And the moun-tains in re-ply, Ech-o-ing their joy-ous strain.

REFRAIN

f "Glo - - - - - - - - - - ry to

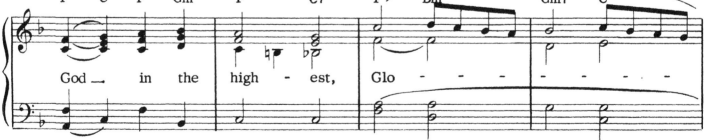

God __ in the high - est, Glo - - - - - - -

- - - - - - ry to God in the High - est" ___

2. Shepherds, why this jubilee?
   Why your joyful strains prolong?
   What the gladsome tidings be
   Which inspire your heav'nly song?
   Refrain

3. Come to Bethlehem and see
   Him whose birth the angels sing:
   Come adore on bended knee
   Christ, the Lord, the newborn King.
   Refrain

4. See Him in a manger laid,
   Whom the choirs of angels praise;
   Holy Spirit, lend thine aid,
   While our hearts in love we raise.
   Refrain

As with Gladness, Men of Old

Words by William C. Dix
Music by Konrad Kocher

Moderately

3. As they offered gifts most rare
   At that manger, rude and bare,
   So may we with holy joy,
   Pure, and free from sin's alloy,
   All our costliest treasures bring,
   Christ, to Thee, our heavenly King.

4. Holy Jesus, every day
   Keep us in the narrow way;
   And, when earthly things are past,
   Bring our ransomed souls at last
   Where they need no star to guide,
   Where no clouds Thy glory hide.

5. In the heav'nly country bright
   Need they no created light:
   Thou its light, its joy, its crown,
   Thou its sun which goes not down:
   There forever may we sing
   Alleluias to our King.

Away in a Manger

Traditional words
Music by James R. Murray

2. The cattle are lowing, the baby awakes,
   But little Lord Jesus, no crying He makes.
   I love thee, Lord Jesus, look down from the sky,
   And stay by my cradle till morning is nigh.

3. Be near me Lord Jesus, I ask thee to stay
   Close by me forever, and love me, I pray.
   Bless all the dear children in Thy tender care,
   And fit us for heaven to live with Thee there.

Behold That Star

American Christmas spiritual

Moderately

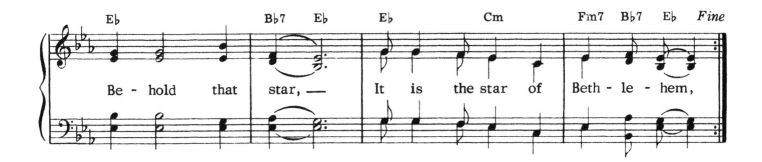

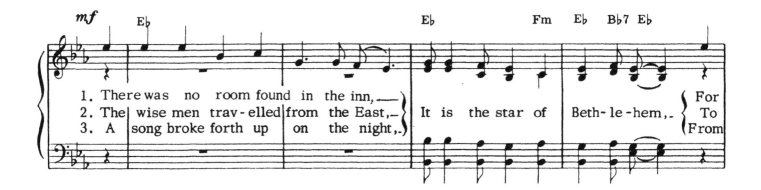

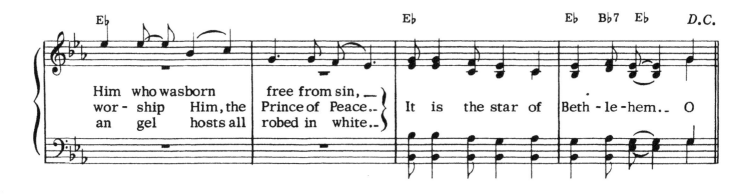

Christ Was Born on Christmas Day

German carol

Moderately

1. Christ was born on Christ - mas Day, Wreathe the hol - ly,
2. He is born to set us free, He is born, our

twine the bay: *Christ - us na - tus ho - di - e,* The
lord to be: *Ex Mar - i - a Vir - gin - e,* The

Babe, the Son, the Ho - ly One of Mar - y.
God, the Lord, by all a - dored for - ev - er.

3. Let the bright red berries glow
Everywhere in goodly show:
Christus natus hodie
The Babe, the Son, the Holy One of Mary.

4. Christian men, rejoice and sing
'Tis the birthday of a king:
Ex Maria Virgine
The God, the Lord, by all adored forever.

Christians Awake

Words by John Byrom
Music by John Wainright

Moderately

1. Christ-ians, a - wake, sa - lute the hap-py morn, Where-on the
2. Then to the watch - ful shep-herds it was told, Who heard th'an-

Sa - vior of man - kind was born; Rise to a - dore the mas-ter-y of
gel - ic her - ald's voice: "Be - hold, I bring good tid - ings of a Sa - vior's

love, Which hosts of an- gels chant-ed from a - bove; With them the joy - ful
birth To you and all the na-tions up - on earth; This day hath God ful -

tid - ings first be - gun __ Of God In - car-nate and the Vir - gin's __ Son.
filled His prom-ised word, __ This day is born a Sa - vior, Christ, the __ Lord.

3. He spake, and straightway the celestial choir,
In hymns of joy, unknown before conspire:
The praises of redeeming love they sang,
And heav'n's whole arch with Alleluias rang,
God's highest glory was their anthem still,
Peace upon earth, and unto men good will.

4. To Bethl'hem straight the happy shepherds ran,
To see the wonder God had wrought for man:
And found, with Joseph and the blessed Maid,
Her Son, the Savior, in a manger laid,
Amazed, the wondrous story they proclaim,
The earliest heralds of the Savior's name.

Coventry Carol

English carol

3. Herod the king, in his raging,
   Charged he hath this day
   His men of might, in his own sight,
   All children young to slay.

4. Then woe is me, poor Child, for Thee,
   And ever morn and day,
   For Thy parting nor say nor sing,
   Bye, bye, lully, lullay.

The First Nowell

English carol

Moderately

1. The___ first___ Now ell the___ an - gel did
2. They___ look - ed___ up and___ saw___ a

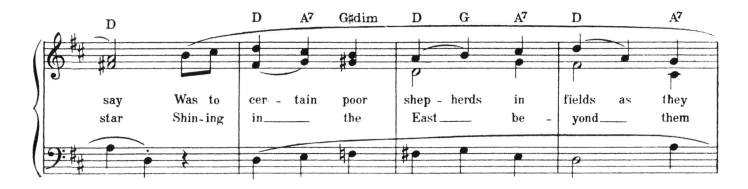

say Was to cer - tain poor shep - herds in fields as they
star Was Shin - ing in___ the East___ be - yond___ them

lay, In___ fields___ where___ they lay___ keep - ing their
far, And___ to___ the___ earth it___ gave___ great

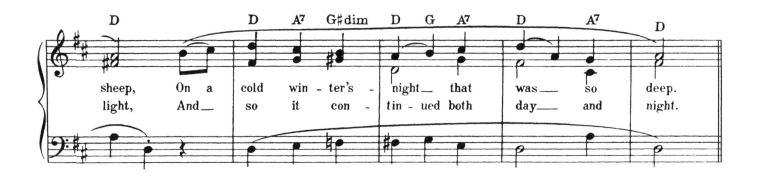

sheep, On a cold win - ter's - night___ that was___ so deep.
light, And___ so it con - tin - ued both day___ and night.

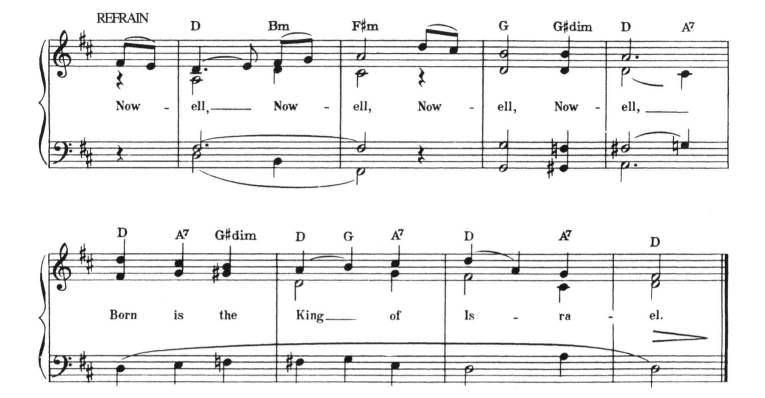

REFRAIN

Now - ell,_____ Now - ell, Now - ell, Now - ell,_____

Born is the King_____ of Is - ra - el.

3. And by the light of that same star
Three wise men came from country far;
To seek for a king was their intent
And to follow the star wheresoever it went.
Refrain

4. The star drew nigh to the Northwest,
O'er Bethlehem it took its rest,
And there it did both stop and stay,
Right over the place where Jesus lay.
Refrain

5. Then entered in those wisemen three,
Full rev'rently upon the knee,
And offered there in His presence,
Their gold and myrrh and frankincense.
Refrain

6. Then let us all with one accord
Sing praises to our heavenly Lord
That hath made heaven and earth of naught
And with His blood mankind hath bought.
Refrain

Good King Wenceslas

Words by John M. Neale
Swedish carol

Moderately fast

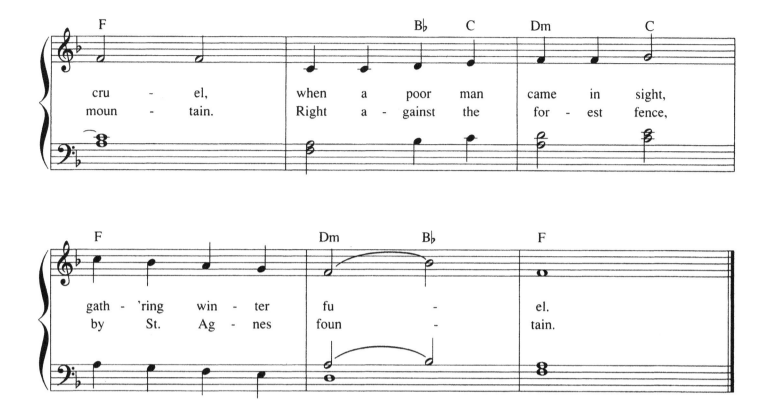

cru - el, / moun - tain.
when a poor man / Right a - gainst the
came in sight, / for - est fence,

gath - 'ring win - ter / by St. Ag - nes
fu - / foun -
el. / tain.

3. "Bring me flesh, and bring me wine,
Bring me pinelogs hither;
Thou and I shall see him dine
When we bear them thither."
Page and monarch forth they went,
Forth they went together:
Through the rude wind's wild lament
And the bitter weather.

4. "Sire, the night is darker now,
And the wind blows stronger;
Fails my heart, I know not how,
I can go no longer."
"Mark my footsteps good, my page,
Tread thou in them boldly.
Thou shalt find the winter's rage
Freeze thy blood less coldly."

5. In his master's steps he trod,
Where the snow lay dinted;
Heat was in the very sod
Which the saint had printed.
Therefore, Christian men be sure,
Wealth or rank possessing,
Ye who now will bless the poor,
Shall yourselves find blessing.

Go Tell It on the Mountain

American Christmas spiritual

With movement

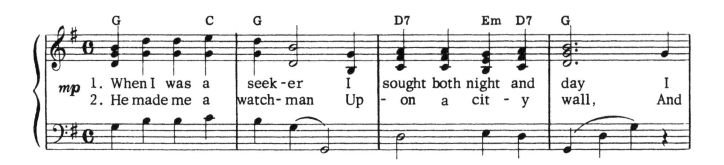

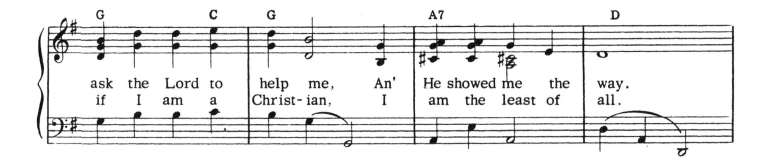

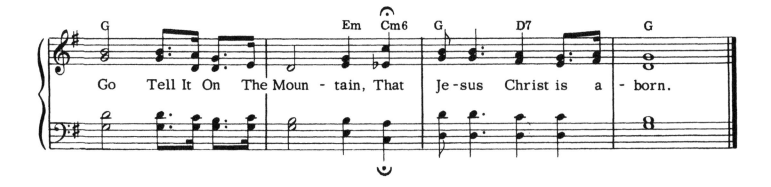

The Holy Babe

Words by Edward Caswall
Music by John B. Dykes

Slowly

1. Sleep, Ho - ly Babe! Up - on Thy__ moth - er's breast; Great

Lord of earth, and sea and sky, How sweet it is to__ see Thee lie In

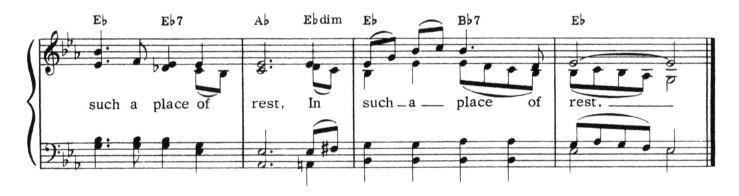

such a place of rest, In such__ a__ place of rest._____

2. Sleep, Holy Babe; Thine angels watch around,
   All bending low with folded wings,
   Before th'Incarnate King of Kings,
   In rev'rent awe profound.
   In rev'rent awe profound.

3. Sleep, Holy Babe! While I with Mary gaze,
   In joy upon that face awhile,
   Upon the loving infant smile,
   Which there divinely plays,
   Which there divinely plays.

4. Sleep, Holy Babe! Ah, take Thy brief repose;
   Too quickly will Thy slumbers break,
   And Thou to lengthened pain awake,
   That Death alone shall close,
   That Death alone shall close.

Hark! the Herald Angels Sing

Words by Charles Wesley
Music by Felix Mendelssohn

Majestically

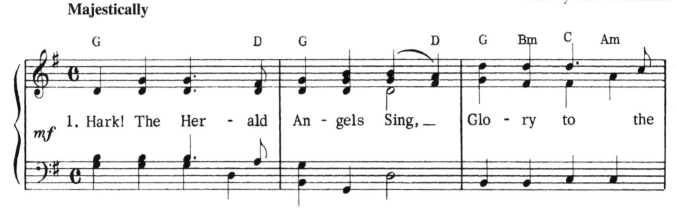

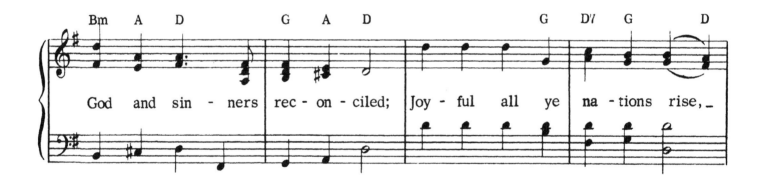

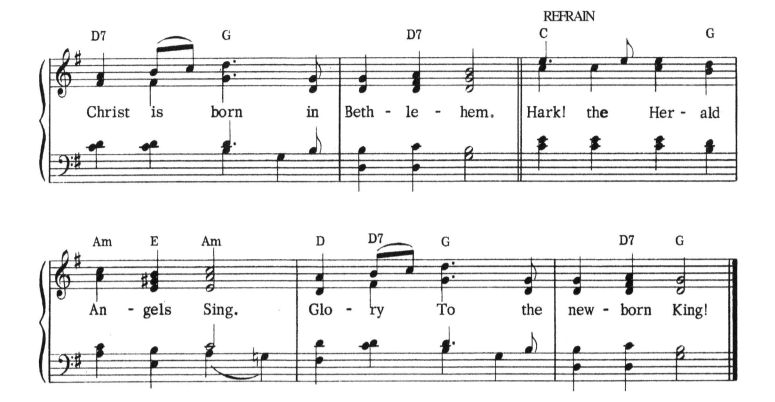

Christ is born in Beth - le - hem. Hark! the Her - ald

An - gels Sing. Glo - ry To the new - born King!

2. Christ, by highest heaven adored;
   Christ, the everlasting Lord;
   Late in time behold Him come,
   Offspring of the Virgin's womb.
   Veiled in flesh the Godhead see;
   Hail th'Incarnate Deity,
   Pleased as man with man to dwell;
   Jesus, our Emmanuel.
   Refrain

3. Hail the heavenborn Prince of Peace!
   Hail the Sun of Righteousness!
   Light and life to all He brings,
   Risen with healing in His wings;
   Mild He lays His glory by,
   Born that man no more may die,
   Born to raise the sons of earth,
   Born to give them second birth.
   Refrain

I Saw Three Ships

English carol

Moderately fast

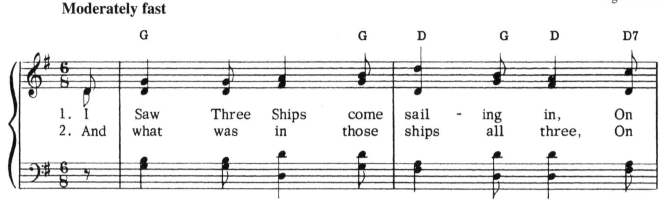

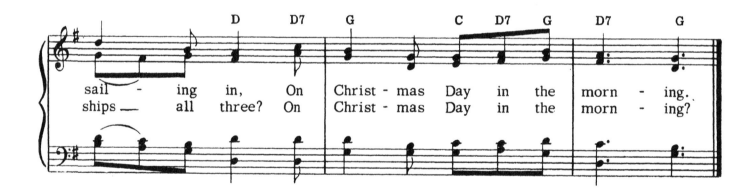

3. The Virgin Mary and Christ was there,
   On Christmas Day, on Christmas Day.
   The Virgin Mary and Christ was there,
   On Christmas Day in the morning.

4. Then let us all rejoice amain,
   On Christmas Day, on Christmas Day.
   Then let us all rejoice amain,
   On Christmas Day in the morning.

Joy to the World

Words by Isaac Watts
English air "Antioch"

Majestically

2. Joy to the world! The Savior reigns;
   Let men their songs employ;
   While fields and floods, rocks, hills and plains
   Repeat the sounding joy,
   Repeat the sounding joy,
   Repeat, repeat the sounding joy.

3. He rules the world with truth and grace,
   And makes the nations prove
   The glories of His righteousness,
   And wonders of His love,
   And wonders of His love,
   And wonders, wonders of His love.

It Came upon the Midnight Clear

Words by Edmund H. Sears
Music by Richard S. Willis

Moderately

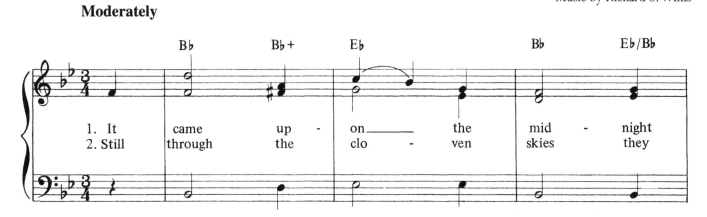

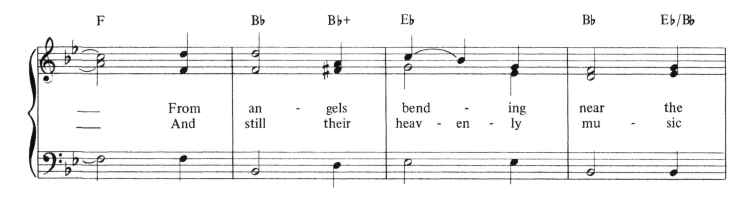

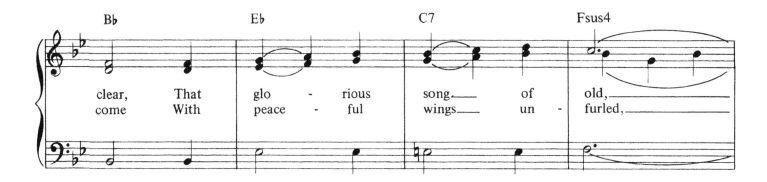

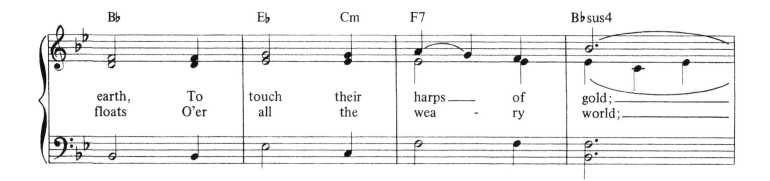

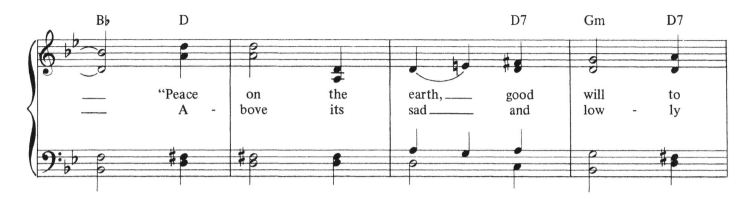

"Peace on the earth,___ good will to
A - bove its sad___ and low - ly

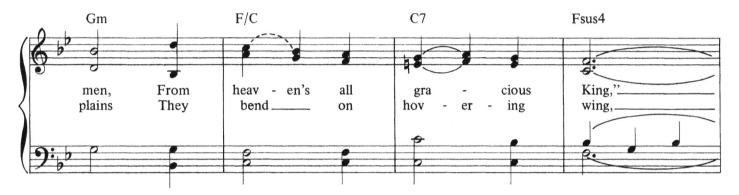

men, From heav - en's all gra - cious King,"___
plains They bend___ on hov - er - ing wing,___

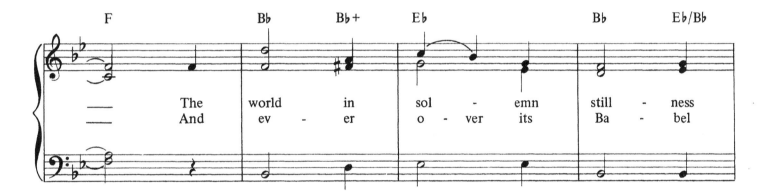

The world in sol - emn still - ness
And ev - er o - ver its Ba - bel

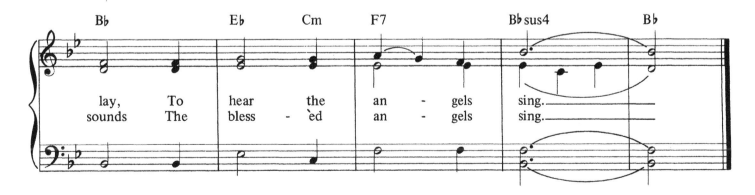

lay, To hear the an - gels sing.
sounds The bless - `ed an - gels sing.___

3. And ye, beneath life's crushing load,
   Whose forms are bending low,
   Who toil along the climbing way
   With painful steps and slow,
   Look now! for glad and golden hours
   Come swiftly on the wing.
   O rest bside the weary road,
   And hear the angels sing!

4. For lo! the days are hastening on,
   By prophet-bards foretold,
   When with the ever circling years
   Comes round the age of gold;
   When peace shall over all the earth
   Its ancient splendors fling,
   And the whole world send back the song
   Which now the angels sing.

Mary Had a Baby

American Christmas spiritual

3. Laid Him in a manger, oh, Lord,
   Laid Him in a manger, oh, Lord,
   Laid Him in a manger, laid Him in a manger,
   Laid Him in a manger, oh Lord.

4. What did she name Him? oh, Lord,
   What did she name Him? oh, Lord,
   What did she name Him? What did she name Him?
   What did she name Him? oh, Lord.

5. Named Him King Jesus, oh, Lord,
   Named Him King Jesus, oh, Lord,
   Named Him King Jesus, named Him King Jesus,
   Named Him King Jesus, oh, Lord.

6. Who heard the singing? oh, Lord,
   Who heard the singing? oh, Lord,
   Who heard the singing? Who heard the singing?
   Who heard the singing? oh, Lord.

7. Shepherds heard the singing, oh, Lord,
   Shepherds heard the singing, oh, Lord,
   Shepherds heard the singing, shepherds heard the singing,
   Shepherds heard the singing, oh, Lord.

8. Star kept a-shining, oh, Lord,
   Star kept a-shining, oh, Lord,
   Star kept a-shining, star kept a-shining,
   Star kept a-shining, oh, Lord.

O Come All Ye Faithful

English carol

With movement

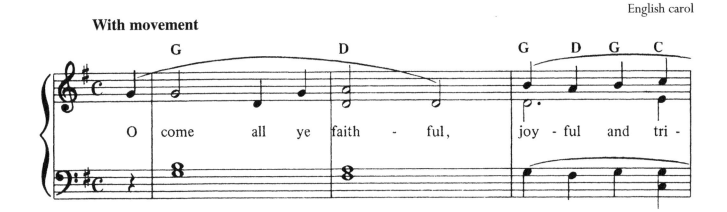

O come all ye faith - ful, joy - ful and tri -

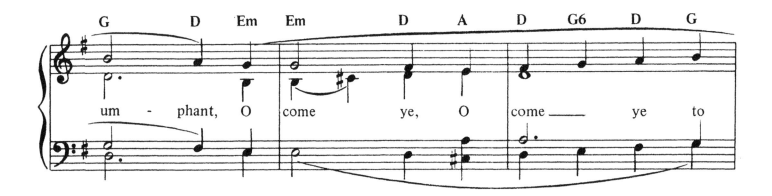

um - phant, O come ye, O come ___ ye to

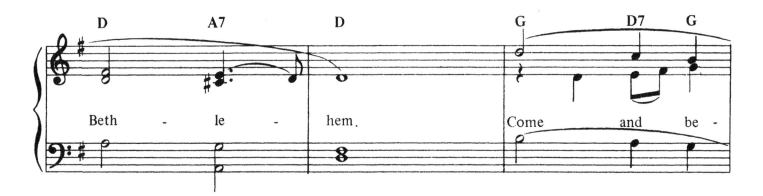

Beth - le - hem. Come and be -

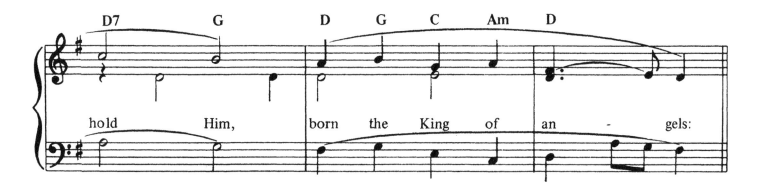

hold Him, born the King of an - gels:

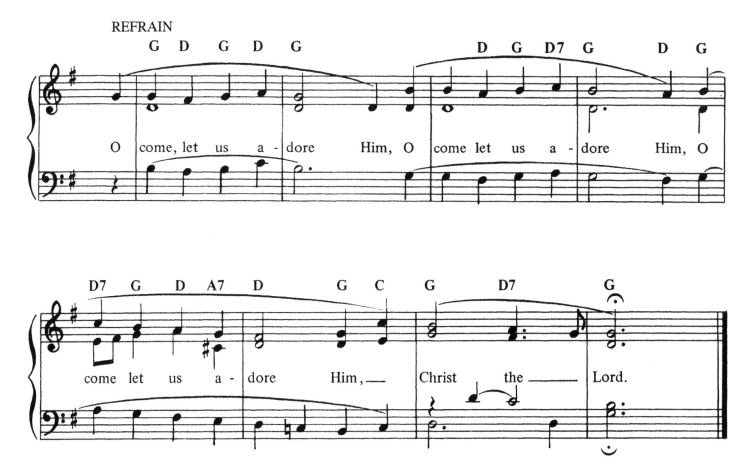

REFRAIN

O come, let us a-dore Him, O come let us a-dore Him, O come let us a-dore Him,— Christ the Lord.

2. Sing, choirs of angels, sing in exultation,
   O sing all ye citizens of heaven above!
   Glory to God, all Glory in the highest.
   Refrain

3. Child, for us sinners, poor and in the manger,
   We would embrace Thee, with love and awe;
   Who would not love Thee, loving us so dearly?
   Refrain

4. Yea, Lord, we greet Thee, born this happy morning,
   Jesus, to Thee be all glory giv'n;
   Word of the Father, now in flesh appearing.
   Refrain

O Come, O Come Immanuel

French carol

Moderately

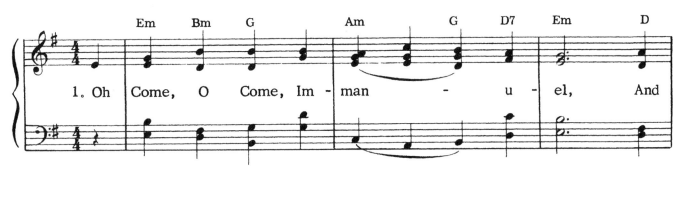

1. Oh Come, O Come, Im - man - u - el, And

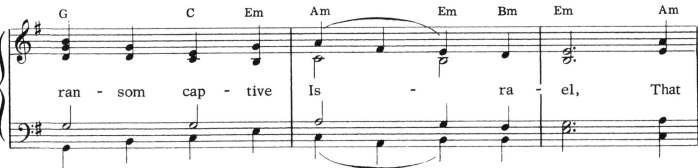

ran - som cap - tive Is - ra - el, That

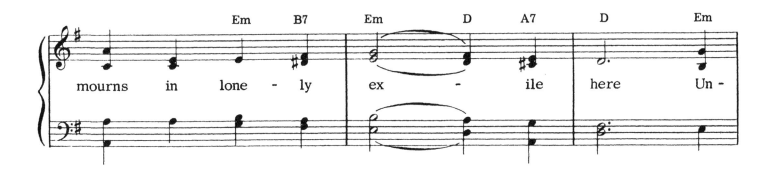

mourns in lone - ly ex - ile here Un -

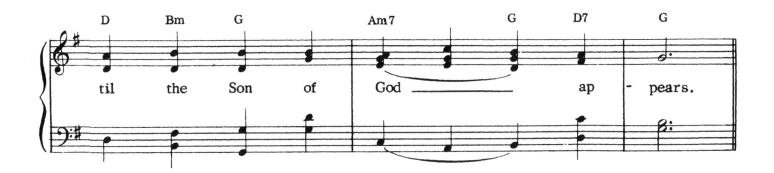

til the Son of God _____ ap - pears.

REFRAIN

Re - joice! Re - joice! Im - man - u - el Shall come to thee O Is - ra - el.

2. O come, O come, Thou rod of Jesse, free
Thine own from Satan's tyranny,
From depths of hell thy people save,
And give them victr'y o'er the grave.
Refrain

3. O come, Thou Day-Spring, come and cheer
Our spirits by Thine advent here,
Disperse the gloomy clouds of night,
And death's dark shadows put to flight.
Refrain

4. O come, Thou key of David come,
And open wide our heav'nly home,
Make safe the way that leads on high,
And close the path to misery.
Refrain

O Holy Night

Words by John Sullivan Dwight
Music by Adolphe Adam

Moderately slow

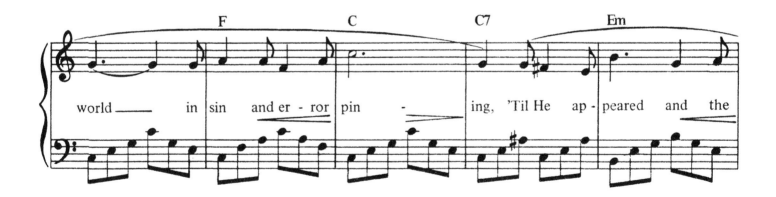

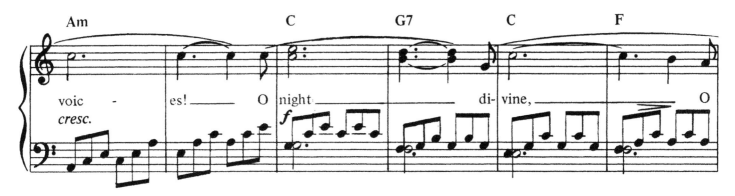

O Little Town of Bethlehem

Words by Phillips Brooks
Music by Lewis H. Redner

Moderately

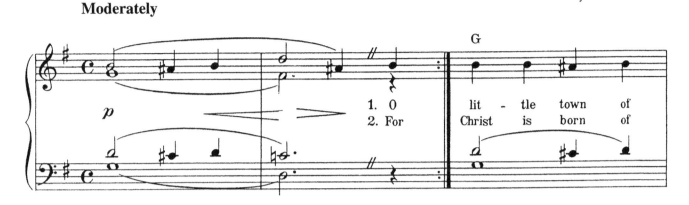

1. O
2. For

lit - tle town of
Christ is born of

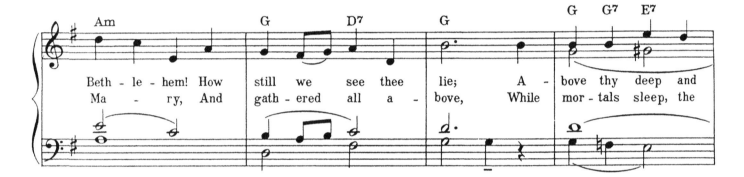

Beth - le - hem! How still we see thee lie; A - bove thy deep and
Ma - ry, And gath - ered all a - bove, While mor - tals sleep, the

dream - less sleep The si - lent stars go by; Yet in thy dark streets
an - gels keep Their watch of won - d'ring love. O morn - ing stars, to

shin - eth The ev - er - last - ing light: The hopes and fears of
geth - er Pro - claim the ho - ly birth! And prais - es sing to

all the years Are met in thee to night. For el
God the King, And peace to men on earth!

3. How silently, how silently,
   The wondrous gift is giv'n!
   So God imparts to human hearts
   The blessings of His heav'n.
   No ear may hear His coming,
   But in this world of sin,
   When meek souls will receive Him, still
   The dear Christ enters in.

4. O Holy Child of Bethlehem!
   Descend to us, we pray;
   Cast out our sin, and enter in;
   Be born in us today.
   We hear the Christmas angels
   The great glad tidings tell;
   O come to us, abide with us
   Our Lord Emmanuel.

Rise Up, Shepherd, an' Follow

American Christmas spiritual

Moderately

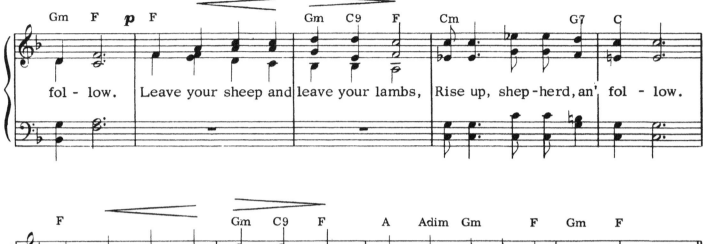

fol - low. Leave your sheep and leave your lambs, Rise up, shep-herd, an' fol - low.

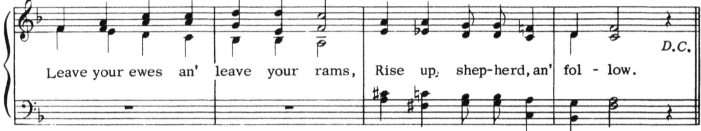

Leave your ewes an' leave your rams, Rise up, shep-herd, an' fol - low.

D.C.

Silent Night

Words by Joseph Mohr
Music by Franz Xaver Gruber

Gently

1. Si - lent night, ho - ly night,
2. Si - lent night, ho - ly night,

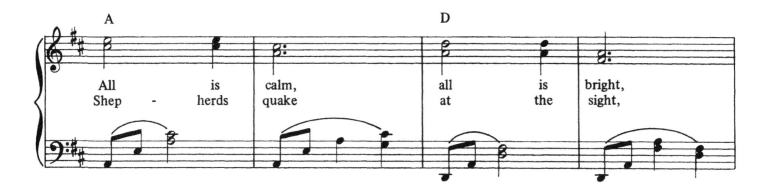

All is calm, all is bright,
Shep - herds quake at the sight,

Round yon vir - gin moth - er and child.
Glo - ries stream from heav - en a - far.

Ho - ly in - fant so ten - der and mild,
Heav - enly hosts sing al - le - lu - ia

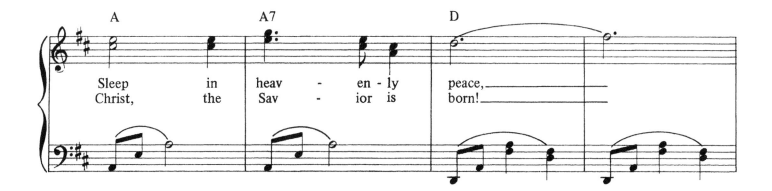

Sleep in heav - en - ly peace,_____
Christ, the Sav - ior is born!_____

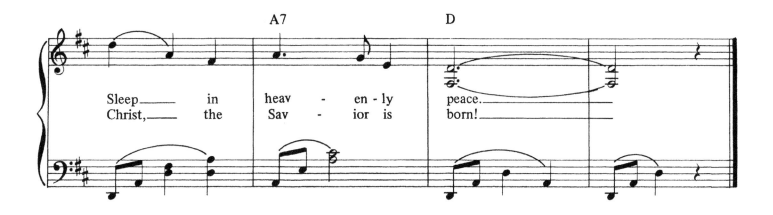

Sleep_____ in heav - en - ly peace._____
Christ,_____ the Sav - ior is born!_____

3. Silent night, holy night,
 Sun of God, love's pure light,
 Radiant beams from Thy holy face,
 With the dawn of redeeming grace,
 Jesus, Lord at Thy birth,
 Jesus, Lord at Thy birth,

4. Silent night, holy night,
 Wondrous star, lend thy light;
 With the angels let us sing
 Alleluia to our king,
 Christ, the Savior, is born.
 Christ, the Savior, is born.

We Three Kings

Words and music by John H. Hopkins, Jr.

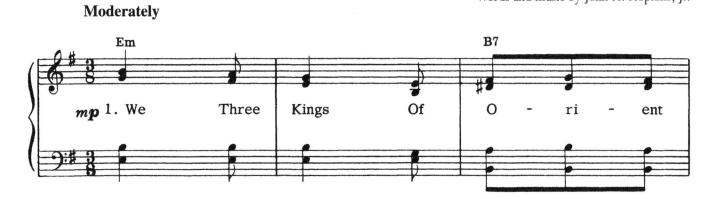

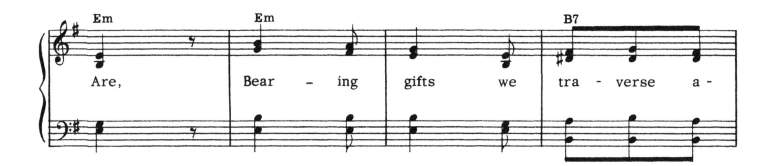

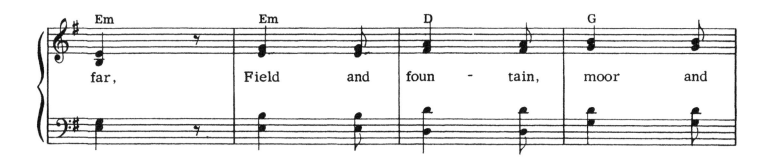

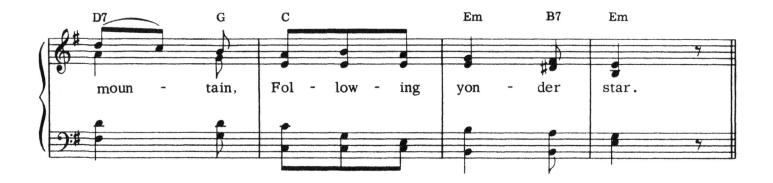

REFRAIN

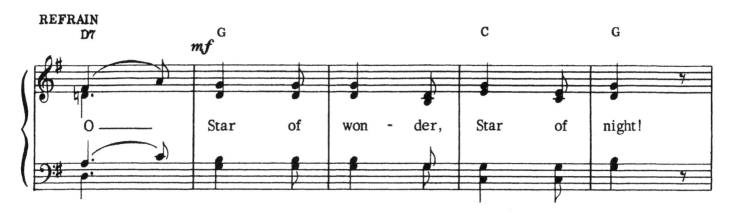

O —— Star of won - der, Star of night!

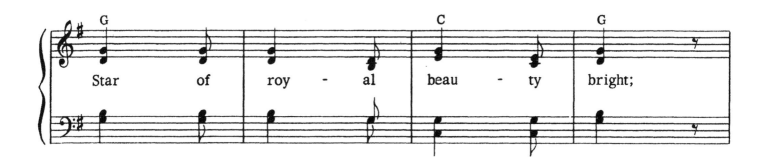

Star of roy - al beau - ty bright;

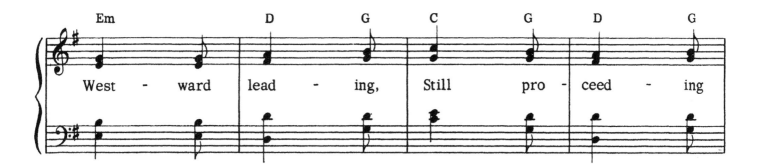

West - ward lead - ing, Still pro - ceed - ing

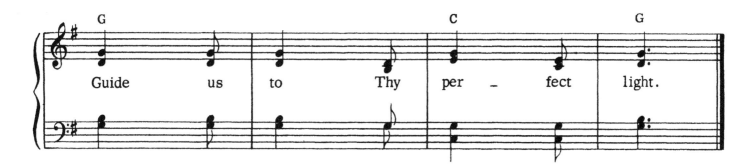

Guide us to Thy per - fect light.

2. Born a King on Bethlehem plain,
   Gold I bring to crown Him again,
   King forever, ceasing never,
   Over us all to reign.
   Refrain

3. Frankincense to offer have I,
   Incense owns a Deity nigh:
   Prayer and praising, all men raising,
   Worship Him, God on high.
   Refrain

4. Myrrh is mine; its bitter perfume
   Breathes a life of gathering gloom;
   Sorrowing, sighing, bleeding, dying,
   Sealed in the stone cold tomb.
   Refrain

5. Glorious now behold Him arise,
   King and God, and sacrifice;
   Heaven sings Alleluia:
   Alleluia the earth replies.
   Refrain

Auld Lang Syne

(New Year's Anthem)

Words by Robert Burns
Scottish air

Moderately slow

3. We twa ha'e ran aboot the braes,
And pu'd the gowans fine,
We've wandered many a weary foot,
Sin auld lang syne.

4. We twa ha'e sported i' the burn,
Frae mornin' sun till dine,
But seas between us braid ha'e roared,
Sin auld lang syne.

Ring Out, Wild Bells

Words by Alfred, Lord Tennyson
Music by Wolfgang Amadeus Mozart

Brightly

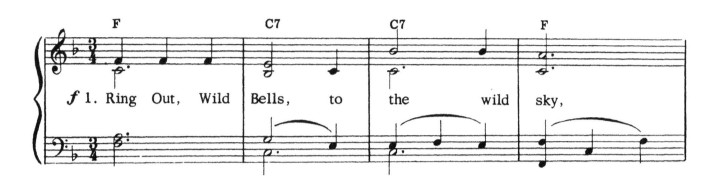

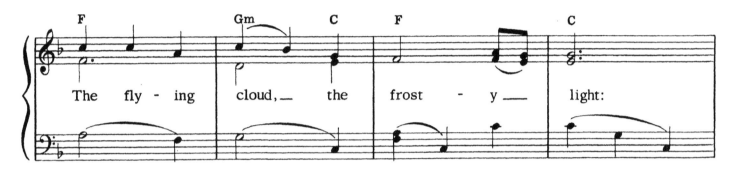

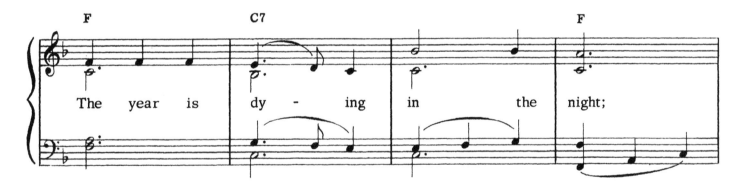

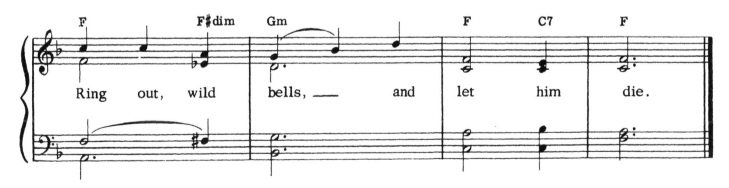

2. Ring out the old, ring in the new,
Ring, happy bells, across the snow:
The year is going, let him go;
Ring out the false, ring in the true.

3. Ring out false pride in place and blood,
The civic slander and the spite;
Ring in the love of truth and right,
Ring in the common love of good.

INDEX